Take C
Your Fertility

Teach Yourself®

Take Charge of Your Fertility

Heather Welford

DISCLAIMER

You're solely responsible for the way you view and use the information in this book, and do so at your own risk. The author and publisher are not responsible in any way for any kind of injuries or health problems that might occur due to using this book or following the advice in it.

For UK order enquiries: please contact
Bookpoint Ltd, 130 Milton Park, Abingdon, Oxon OX14 4SB.
Telephone: +44 (0) 1235 827720. *Fax:* +44 (0) 1235 400454.
Lines are open 09.00–17.00, Monday to Saturday, with a 24-hour message answering service. Details about our titles and how to order are available at www.teachyourself.com

Long renowned as the authoritative source for self-guided learning – with more than 50 million copies sold worldwide – the **Teach Yourself** series includes over 500 titles in the fields of languages, crafts, hobbies, business, computing and education.

British Library Cataloguing in Publication Data:
a catalogue record for this title is available from the British Library.

First published in UK 2007 by Hodder Education,
part of Hachette UK, 338 Euston Road, London NW1 3BH.

This edition published 2010.

Previously published as *Teach Yourself Getting Pregnant*.

The **Teach Yourself** name is a registered trade mark of Hodder Headline.

Typeset by Macmillan Publishing Solutions.

Printed in Great Britain for Hodder Education, an Hachette UK Company, 338 Euston Road, London NW1 3BH, by CPI Cox & Wyman, Reading, Berkshire RG1 8EX.

The publisher has used its best endeavours to ensure that the URLs for external websites referred to in this book are correct and active at the time of going to press. However, the publisher and the author have no responsibility for the websites and can make no guarantee that a site will remain live or that the content will remain relevant, decent or appropriate.

Hachette UK's policy is to use papers that are natural, renewable and recyclable products and made from wood grown in sustainable forests. The logging and manufacturing processes are expected to conform to the environmental regulations of the country of origin.

Impression number	10 9 8 7 6 5 4 3 2 1
Year	2014 2013 2012 2011 2010

Acknowledgements

Thank you to all the people who responded so kindly to my requests for help with this book. In particular, I thank the Miscarriage Association, the National Childbirth Trust and the friends and colleagues who put me in touch with people they knew might be interested in sharing their stories.

Heather Welford, 2010

Contents

Meet the author

Welcome to *Take Charge of Your Fertility*!

So you're planning a pregnancy? Whether you want to get pregnant now or in the near future, whether you have been pregnant before or not, this book will help with practical information about male and female physiology, and give you encouragement, support and details of how you can enhance your chances of conception and having a successful pregnancy.

There's information about when and how to seek medical help, and a peek at some of the assistance you can get from medical technology. Real life experience forms an important part of the text too, to ensure the emotional and social sides of this important journey get their due attention. There are links to current internet forums and support groups which put parents and would-be parents in touch with each other.

Biomedical science pushes at boundaries every day; books can't hope to keep pace with the very latest intervention, laws or current practice. In most cases, if becoming pregnant doesn't 'just happen' when you want it to, small changes in timing, preparation and forethought are worth trying, and for most healthy couples are all that's needed. This book shares them with you, together with information on how to be fit and healthy at conception and early pregnancy.

I first met concerns around fertility when I worked for *Parents* magazine (now long defunct) many years ago. With a small team of obstetricians and other medics, I answered readers' requests for advice, and 'Help, I want to get pregnant' was always one of the most common of them. Since then I've had my own three children, and while I have not faced worries about delays in pregnancy or difficulties in sustaining a pregnancy myself, I've been close to a number of people who have, and I have seen close up that it affects mental and emotional well-being and relationships. As a journalist, I've interviewed a number of individuals and couples whose lives have been touched by fertility issues. This book has allowed me to explore these issues from all angles, and I hope it helps bring a practical and sympathetic perspective to them.

Heather Welford

Only got a minute?

If you're planning a pregnancy, even if you know it may not be for some time, getting to know your options and exploring your choices will help you take control.

You need to think about:

▶ your relationship

▶ your health

▶ your partner's health

▶ your age and your partner's age

▶ how you can assess your fertility

▶ how you can schedule sex to make the most of your fertile time.

Understanding how conception happens and how early pregnancy develops allows you to appreciate the different ways you can take control of your reproductive health and outcomes. Technology is on your side, and home-use assessment and kits are inexpensive and reliable. Pregnancy testing is also easy and cheap to do, and gives results very quickly. This means you will be aware of pregnancy confirmation earlier than ever before.

You can also increase your chances of having a healthy, enjoyable pregnancy. If you have difficulties getting or staying pregnant, find out more about when to seek medical help and what this can offer you. Be aware that all of these circumstances and experiences may have an emotional impact on you and your partner, and that you will need each other's support at times.

If you experience pregnancy loss, you may want to find out more about the causes, or you may need to accept there is no one way of pinpointing a cause. This may be a challenge, and take time for you to accept and move on.

5 Only got five minutes?

If you're planning a pregnancy, even if you know it may not be for some time, getting to know your options and exploring your choices will help you take control. You can leave it all up to nature if you want to, but you don't have to. The trend today is to have children later, perhaps waiting for professional, financial and personal circumstances to feel right. However, delaying for several years, whatever the reason, may mean that you are not giving nature much of a helping hand.

It's important to consider your circumstances, and to be prepared for the big changes in your life that come with having children.

You need to discuss and become aware of the implications of:

▶ *your relationship*
▶ *your health*
▶ *your partner's health*
▶ *your age and your partner's age.*

You can also learn more about:

▶ *how you can assess your fertility*
▶ *how you can schedule sex to make the most of your fertile time.*

Women's fertility is very much affected by age. The easiest age to get pregnant – that is, the time when ovulation happens reliably and with 'good quality' eggs – is in the 20s. After the age of 30, fertility starts to decline, and it takes a further dip after the age of 35, and then again after the age of 40.

Men's fertility declines too, but not in the same, very marked way as women's. Both sexes' ages have an impact on pregnancy outcomes.

These issues are not resolvable by freezing eggs, sperm or embryos for later use and it's unrealistic to expect these innovations to help any more than a very few people in special circumstances, at least for the near future.

Understanding fertility rather than pinning hopes on new technology will help you make decisions more realistically, and decide what the issues mean to you as individuals.

You can start by understanding how conception happens and how early pregnancy develops, which allows you to appreciate the different ways you can take control of your reproductive health and its outcomes. Technology for assessing this is on your side, and home-use kits are inexpensive and reliable. Pregnancy testing is also easy and cheap to do, and gives results very quickly. This means you will be aware of pregnancy confirmation earlier than ever before.

You can also increase your chances of having a healthy, enjoyable pregnancy. If you have difficulties getting or staying pregnant, find out more about when to seek medical help and what this can offer you. Be aware that all of these circumstances and experiences may have an emotional impact on you and your partner, and that you will need each other's support at times.

If you experience pregnancy loss, you may want to find out more about the causes, or you may need to accept there is no one way of pinpointing a cause. This may be a challenge, and take time for you to accept and move on.

10 Only got ten minutes?

If you're planning a pregnancy, even if you know it may not be for some time, getting to know your options and exploring your choices will help you take control. You can leave it all up to nature if you want to, but you don't have to, once you are aware that you can make small changes to your routine to maximize your chances of conception and pregnancy.

The trend today is to have children later, perhaps waiting for professional, financial and personal circumstances to feel right. However, delaying for several years, whatever the reason, may mean that you are not giving nature much of a helping hand. Delaying pregnancy can lead to interventions which are far from guaranteed, and can be expensive, uncomfortable and stressful.

You need to know that about one in five couples has difficulty in getting pregnant, and while most do conceive successfully and go on to have a healthy pregnancy and a healthy child, the road can be rocky and sometimes distressing. No one can tell you when you 'should' have children, but biological timing should be part of your decision-making.

Considering all your circumstances helps you be prepared for the big changes in your life that come with having children.

You need to discuss and become aware of the implications of:

▶ *your relationship*
▶ *your health*
▶ *your partner's health*
▶ *your age and your partner's age.*

You can also learn more about:

▶ *how you can assess your fertility*
▶ *how you can schedule sex to make the most of your fertile time.*

Women's fertility is, as we know, very much affected by age. The easiest age to get pregnant – that is, the time when ovulation happens reliably and with 'good quality' eggs – is in the 20s. After the age of 30, fertility starts to decline, and it takes a further dip after the age of 35, and again after the age of 40. It's a feature of our society that many people, especially women, don't feel ready, or with the right person, at the time nature would 'prefer' them to go for it.

Men's fertility declines too, but not in the same, very marked way as women's. Both sexes' ages have an impact on pregnancy outcomes.

These issues are not resolvable by freezing eggs, sperm or embryos for later use, despite the breakthroughs read about in the newspapers, and it's unrealistic to expect these innovations to help any more than a very few people in special circumstances, at least for the near future. In addition, even more established forms of assisted reproduction like IVF or ICSI fail far more often than they succeed. Donor eggs and donor sperm have their own issues and potential problems too, as does surrogacy – though all these options have brought happy results for many people. Complementary and alternative medicine and treatment may appear alluring, but most of it is untested and unproved, and some types may even undermine fertility.

Understanding fertility rather than pinning hopes on new technology will help you make decisions more realistically, and decide what the issues all mean to you as individuals.

You can start with understanding how conception happens and how early pregnancy develops, which allows you to appreciate the different ways you can take control of your reproductive health and its outcomes. Technology for assessing this, for both men and women, is on your side, and home-use kits are inexpensive and reliable, with innovations happening all the time. Pregnancy testing is also easy and cheap to do, and gives results very quickly. This means you will be aware of pregnancy confirmation earlier than ever before.

You can also increase your chances of having a healthy, enjoyable pregnancy. If you have difficulties getting or staying pregnant, find out more about when to seek medical help and what this can offer you. Be aware that all of these circumstances and experiences may have an emotional impact on you and your partner, and that you will need each other's support at times. Finding support outside your relationship can be good too. Internet forums and support groups in real life, perhaps connected with clinics, allow you to share and offer support with people going through similar experiences. This can bring you hope and strength.

If you experience pregnancy loss, you may want to find out more about the causes, or you may need to accept there is no way of pinpointing a cause. This may be a challenge, and it may take time for you to accept what has happened, and move on.

Introduction

You're reading this not because you don't know where babies come from – but because it isn't happening for you at the moment, or else because you think you might want to become pregnant in the future.

This book will help you focus on the questions you might ask yourself about timing. For instance, is there a good time to become pregnant for you, and your life? What are the ways in which your age, or the age of your partner, can impact on your choice?

You'll discover the way biology works to help or hinder you.

Women are able to conceive on only a few days every month, and sexual intercourse outside those times won't end in pregnancy. Even healthy, fertile women have only about a one in four chance of conceiving in any one month, even if they are having sex at the best time. This book will help you work out how you can use a better knowledge of the way your body works to achieve a pregnancy, and to have as healthy a pregnancy as you can.

In addition, the book includes an overview of the ways in which conception can be delayed, or prevented, and what can be done to remove the obstacles. Couples who want a baby but are finding it difficult will be helped to work out if there is a physical barrier – something preventing sperm (or enough of them) getting to a stage where they can meet the egg, or something preventing the egg from meeting the sperm – or if sperm and egg are not being released at all.

Becoming pregnant is only part of the story. The book also looks at pregnancy loss and what might lie behind that.

All aspects of conception, pregnancy and birth involve your feelings and those of your partner; the journey to parenthood is an emotional and psychological one. This book will help to answer some of your questions such as: When can you test for pregnancy? What does it feel like? Who should you tell you are pregnant, and when? What's the impact of this knowledge? Also, if you experience delays or disappointments in trying to become a parent, you'll find experiences that echo your own, and which acknowledge the great effect this can have on your relationships and how you feel about yourself.

Support groups of parents, parents-to-be and would-be parents can be important in helping you cope with this journey by sharing friendship, understanding and knowledge. In this internet age, it's easy to find them. On every parenting website, there are forums, talkboards and/or chat rooms, for those members who are 'TTC' (trying to conceive), with many broken down into sub-groups of people going through IVF, surrogacy, trying to add to their family of one, two or more children, those who have experienced pregnancy loss etc.; this networking is the web at its best. You can also use the internet to keep up with medical research and to learn more from the same academic journals doctors read.

The personal experiences in the book are all genuine, and have come from people who were kind enough to speak to me or email me. I used my existing contacts, and contacts from the Miscarriage Association, and I also asked for people to respond to requests on e-groups run by the National Childbirth Trust.

1

The right time?

In this chapter you will learn:
- *how to determine the 'right time'*
- *what choices surround the decision to try for a baby*
- *about the latest information and research on fertility changes.*

Twenty-first century parents – or would-be parents – have a free choice about when to have their families, or at least, that's what it seems like. There's a prevailing idea that it's easy enough to decide when to have a baby, and that when you've decided the time is right, you go ahead and it just happens.

The reality is, however, that the decision-making is hard for many people, and fraught with questions to do with biology, finances, career structure and relationships; and then even if a decision is made, the 'just happens' bit of the process doesn't always work out.

For women, particularly, the crudely termed 'biological clock' is a major issue. Novelist Helen Fielding's modern-day anti-heroine, Bridget Jones, had to cope with her mother's friends making loud and significant 'tick tock tick tock' whispers towards her at family gatherings – and while most women don't have to face that, there are plenty of people willing to remind any woman over 30, if she needed it, that she doesn't have unlimited time available.

Newspaper and magazine articles might include interviews and items about the latest celebrity mother to give birth aged 40-plus – but they're also happy to include regular items on the price women pay for delaying their childbearing, which can be heartache on the emotional side, and huge costs for private fertility treatment on the financial side.

How you decide the time is right for you is bound to be an individual decision, based on many unique circumstances and feelings, but alongside those very personal details, which no one can predict or decide for you, it also makes sense to investigate what medical research tells us about reproductive biology, both male and female. Statistics can't ever predict what's going to happen to you, naturally enough, but they can help to add other information to your decision-making.

Insight

Reading about celebrity pregnancies in magazines can mislead you. Many stars retain the full truth about their late babies for the sake of privacy – they may have needed donated eggs or sperm, or had extensive other assistance.

Your feelings

Do you want a child? Do you 'feel' ready for one? Do you feel you have a choice?

Some women – and men – grow up knowing for certain they will want to be parents some day, and they begin to experience a gap in their lives at some point. That feeling of a gap needing to be filled becomes stronger as time goes on, and it's as if they know in their bones having a baby will make them feel complete. Becoming a parent seems to be part of their identity, part of their destiny, and if the conception proves difficult, or fertility issues emerge, the delay can be very hard to bear.

Other people come to a sudden realization that seems to spring from nowhere in particular – being a parent, having a baby, is something they want, even need, to happen.

Could it be that something's going on in the subconscious, that people are planning for when the time is right without knowing? Or is that sudden feeling truly spontaneous, maybe triggered by seeing someone else with a baby, and feeling unexpected pangs of envy?

Traditionally, there's a patriarchal notion that having someone, probably a male, to continue the family is important, and that men should somehow arrange things so this happens, with a compliant female.

Biological determinism would have us – both males and females – keen to ensure our genes are perpetuated so they continue to populate the planet, and we don't, as an example of the species, die out. In old-fashioned terms, we're continuing the 'blood line', because we're genetically propelled to do so.

Whatever the motivation, social or biological or a mix, the need or longing for a child is a genuine one in many of us, and the expectation that a child will be born is an exciting and joyful one. While not everyone feels strongly that their life will be bleak without their own children, the desire to have a baby, which many people experience, is more than just societal pressure or requests from would-be grandparents to 'get on with it' (though this can make the need more poignant, and fertility problems can be sadder because of what other people expect).

No one can tell you if you're 'correct' in feeling it's the right time to have a baby – that depends on you (and your partner) being honest with yourself and your motivation. No one can ever define the 'right' emotional state for conception, pregnancy and parenthood. It's an individual choice, based on individual motivation.

Case study – Anne

I'd always been the archetypal career woman. At the age of 34, I'd been married for five years and lots of our friends had had babies, but I really never felt broody. In fact, we'd never really talked about having children... then I was made redundant, and used the time not to look for another job but to take time off from the stress of work to do other things, like learning ceramics. It just seemed to clear a space in my head, and led me to think: 'I really want a baby!' Something just clicked, and I knew it was the right moment for us. On our fifth wedding anniversary, we went out for a meal, and I told my husband straight out. His jaw dropped in surprise, but he said: 'OK!' and we went ahead – our daughter was born just under a year later.

Q&A

He wants a baby, and I'm too frightened

Q. I'm scared of childbirth – not just worried about the pain, but totally terrified. I want to be a mother, but the idea of having to go through pregnancy and labour in order to be one is forceful enough to make me prefer not having any children at all.

A. Fear of childbirth is called tokophobia. There are no accurate statistics on how common it is, but it's present in many cultures. One mother told the *Daily Telegraph*: 'I thought I would go mad with the pain and that I'd never recover psychologically.' She was aware of the irrationality of it, 'because other people had babies and lived to tell the tale,' but that made no difference.

Women who have had a baby and who then become frightened, usually because of an unpleasant birth experience, are said to be suffering from 'secondary tokophobia' but in your case, it could be 'primary tokophobia'. You would need to get this diagnosed, and then there would be treatments to explore, such as cognitive behaviour therapy, hypnosis, and maybe thinking about birth options such as a caesarean section, or doing childbirth classes that teach self-hypnosis.

It's certainly strong enough for women to deliberately avoid pregnancy and to even welcome a miscarriage if it happens. But it can be successfully treated.

Insight

Are you sure you want a baby? And that your partner does? Explore your deepest feelings honestly, and don't feel any decision has to be made immediately.

Your partner and your relationship

There's a growing trend for mothers to plan for a go-it-alone pregnancy – a decision is taken to conceive with no expectation of any involvement from the male partner beyond that of providing the sperm. It can also happen that a pregnancy is unexpected and the mother decides not to terminate, without any assumption that her sexual partner will stay around to become a father in the relationship sense of the word.

It's difficult to show this by statistics. In England and Wales, figures from 2001 (from National Statistics at www.statistics. gov.uk) show that 19 per cent of babies born to a single mother were registered by the mother alone (7.3 per cent of all births). But the bald numbers don't show how many of these single mothers were deliberately single or reluctantly single at the time of their babies' birth, how many of them knew the identity of their baby's father but didn't want to share the knowledge, or how many simply preferred for whatever reason not to record the paternity of their child. The statistics also indicate that lone parenthood is associated with disadvantage of various hues – but this is not the book to cover how you can avoid this, or overcome it.

There may be a number of reasons why you feel confident in deciding to become a single parent; or even if you are under-confident, you may feel you can manage to care for your child, or be able to rely on support from family and friends. You may also have ethical objections to terminating an unexpected pregnancy and decide to become a mother for that reason.

Not having a permanent relationship may not appear to be a drawback, or a big enough drawback – but all parents, especially the lone ones, need help, encouragement and a break from time to time. Pregnancy can give you the time to explore support networks, and go some way to filling the gap left by the non-existent partner.

If you're in a close relationship at the time you're considering a pregnancy, the decision to try for a baby is likely to involve the two of you. How do you know your partner is up for it and ready?

The decision to have a baby can be a marker of the strength of your relationship. For many couples, having a baby together is a powerful symbol of their love, and an expression of it; it goes hand in hand with your concern for each other, and feels like a natural progression and maturing of the choice to be together. It's the big, grown-up step you take into adulthood – or that's how it can feel. At the same time, it can seem like a commitment too far for some men (and some women), who recognize (correctly) that having a baby changes priorities forever. If you're happy now, and you feel your life is giving you what you want, why change things? It can feel scary and unpredictable.

Talk about it together and share any doubts you have. Remember that you don't really know how long it will actually take to become pregnant: things could happen immediately, which might make it even more frightening, or it could take some time, and in that time you may find your outlook changes. Some couples find the desire for a baby increases the longer it takes to conceive one. What starts with one partner keener than the other, mutates into a shared and equal need. Wanting a child, with both parents sharing that desire, is a good start for any baby. Occasionally, women take matters in hand and stop using contraception even though their partner has not formally agreed to it, or even when their partner has expressed serious reluctance. Again, there are no statistics on these happy accidents that were not so accidental.

Q&A

He says he doesn't want any kids

Q. How can I persuade my husband that my need for a child is so strong, I'm tempted to go ahead and become pregnant anyway? I've always been in charge of contraception, so it would be easy enough to have an 'accident' – but he is so against the idea, I am scared he would talk about termination. I just don't think he sees himself as a father, and likes his life the way it is now.

A. You can't persuade people to change their mind about something as fundamental as wanting to be a parent, but you can ask your husband to think about it again, and explain how strongly you feel about it. There may be reasons why he feels so strongly the other way – some people have really dreadful childhood memories, and don't want to 'inflict' misery on someone else. Or is there some underlying worry about an inherited disease or condition?

The desire for a child is so powerful that it can come between couples, so it would be worth exploring your options to understand a bit more which one risks a real backlash from your husband.

Case study – Patricia

I wanted babies before he did – I had to work on him. He wasn't keen, and was really taken aback when I actually fell pregnant at 26. I think one good thing about pregnancy lasting as long as it does is that it gives men a chance to get used to the idea, if they were a bit reluctant to start with.

Case study – Caroline

After the first and the second...? As for the third, I would like another baby now, and I try to time the discussions about it when the kids have been wonderful all day and he's had a reasonable night's sleep! Fingers crossed!

Q&A

How will our relationship change?

Q. We're hoping to have a baby soon, but one thing bothers me – I wonder how to keep our relationship going when there's a baby as well. I've observed that friends can find having children brings with it difficult times, and in my own family, I've seen marriages break up after babies come along.

A. You're right not to take anything for granted, and your observations are borne out by research that shows the first year or so after a baby is born can have a negative impact on some couples' relationship. Mental and emotional health issues can appear, and the effects of lack of sleep, maybe lack of money, and the break with life before children all add up to stress and pressure.

On the other hand, while it's very risky to think of babies as having the power to 'save' a poor relationship, they can certainly enhance a good one.

The main advice from parents who cope best with the transition is to make some time for yourselves – this doesn't mean feeling you need to get a babysitter in as soon as your baby is born, or feel pressured to get back to 'normality'. You can make time for yourselves without going out – sometimes you will have to! It means accepting that being loving, sensual and communicative can still happen, even in short bursts, keeping the same supportive, sharing relationship going that led you to want to be life partners.

Insight

The first weeks and months after having a baby are a 'danger time' for relationships. But good, supportive help is available. Bear in mind that men can become depressed and anxious during this period, just like women can.

Your material circumstances

How much does having a baby actually cost?

In 2006, the *Daily Mail* reported estimates that parents-to-be spent an average of £1,560 in the six months before the birth.

▶ *£1,060 went on essentials such as prams, car seats, equipment, baby monitors, toys and clothes.*
▶ *Women spent £500 on clothing, magazines, pampering treatments and health supplements.*

In addition, there was the cost of redecorating, and for one-fifth of new parents, the extra cost of moving house.

According to 2009 calculations published by parenting website gurgle.co.uk, parents spend a staggering £18,000 in the first year, and they add that conception costs can mount up too – pregnancy tests and changes in lifestyle and diet, quite apart from any decision to seek private medical advice on fertility.

There is modest state help for pregnancy-related costs, in the form of the Health in Pregnancy Grant, which is currently non-means-tested and payable after 25 weeks. If you're on a very low income or no income at all, you may get further help. Anyone in work should also get Statutory Maternity Pay or Maternity Allowance. However, none of this is likely to cover all your outgoings.

It's probably not possible to get away with a totally cost-free conception, pregnancy, birth and first year, but if money is tight, then it's not difficult to save money by buying second hand, borrowing and doing without a lot of inessential fripperies.

The question 'Can we afford a baby?' is impossible to answer with a generalization. Feeling financially stable is obviously more comfortable than being on the point of unemployment, or not earning. However, deciding on the 'right time' from a financial point of view will always be subjective too. You may need to decide with your partner on whether you will need two incomes or one, whether you will opt for flexible, part-time or job-share working, and what the impact of this might be on your lifestyle. If you expect to move house, you may also have to factor in any added costs for this. Remember though that babies don't take up a lot of space, and moving to a larger house isn't urgent.

If you see figures telling you that it costs enormous amounts to raise a child, take a deep breath and think: these figures may include university fees and the cost of supporting the 'baby' until age 21. There are many ways to save money – and at this end of your journey, a lot of clothing and equipment is unnecessary, or unnecessarily new: make do uncomplainingly with hand-me-downs and second-hand prams, pushchairs and sleeping places. Babies don't have to be expensive.

An impending 30th birthday can really sharpen your focus...
While such mature pursuits as house-buying, gardening and
having kids still seem some way off, I do sense that they're
creeping closer. Which can really set the mind spiralling.

When it comes to motherhood, for instance, even just
considering it involves weighing up the necessary sacrifices.
And not only those that naturally accompany giving birth to
a tiny creature, entirely dependent on its parents. You also
have to consider those imposed by social opinion.

You have to decide, for instance, whether you're ready to
put your days of doing anything remotely dangerous behind
you, or are prepared to face the alternative – the accusation
of being a bad mother. As far as I can recall, there has rarely
been a major outcry against a father taking on a dangerous
job or challenge, but when a mother embarks on anything
involving acknowledged risks – war reporting, police work,
mountaineering – the criticisms start.

Kira Cochrane, *New Statesman*, 9 April 2007

He says there's no rush

Q. I want a baby, and my partner says there's no rush.
I'm 33 and he's 35. We both have demanding jobs and
a busy social life at weekends. He doesn't want to give this
up, and also says that if we have kids, he would want to
move out to the country, as he thinks the city we live in is
not good for schools – but moving out might mean
changing jobs, as neither of us wants a long commute.

(Contd)

It just seems there's so much to think about, and we should get started now.

A. It sounds as if you've done some talking about how you see your lives with children, so that's a good start. Of course your partner is right – there's no rush, and as pregnancy lasts nine months, you've plenty of time even then to think about moving house and changing jobs – you don't need all those ducks in a row before you start thinking about actually conceiving.

How much do you want a baby now, right this minute (or this year)? Is this something you need to discuss again, to explain to him how strongly you feel? Or would it help just to pin him down to something like 'after a couple more years' or 'after we have found a new house', with a date set for that too?

Time and your fertility

Biology is not very kind to females. While it seems men can have the option of fathering children into old age (though this is probably exaggerated – there's plenty of evidence for declining sperm in men, as you'll see later), women would have to have been living on another planet if they weren't aware of a time limit on their fertility.

In the press – Leaving it too late?

A study shows that some women 'leave it too late', which can lead to childlessness for professional women...

... The findings come from a groundbreaking study into more than 5,000 women born in 1970 and tracked throughout their lives by researchers at the Centre for Longitudinal Studies, based at the Institute of Education in London.

It revealed that 40 per cent of the graduate women were childless at age 35. The researchers forecast that by the time they reach the likely end of their childbearing years at 45, about 30 per cent will still be childless.

Daily Telegraph, 23 April 2007

Women's fertility is probably at its peak between the ages of 20 and 25, and thereafter it starts to decline, slowly at first, and then more markedly from age 35, when the graphs showing aspects of fertility make an 'elbow' shape, taking a visible dip from that point onwards.

▶ *The number of ovarian follicles (where the egg develops) is finite, and obviously starts to fall from the age of menarche (when periods begin). But the drop becomes more marked from age 35, and takes a further sharp dip at age 40.*
▶ *This reduction in ovarian follicles affects how quickly you're likely to become pregnant, once you start having sex without contraception. Between age 30 and 35, fertility is 15–20 per cent below maximum. Between age 35 and 39, the decrease is 25–50 per cent. And between age 40 and 45, the decrease is 50–95 per cent.*
▶ *Miscarriage rate is fairly static through the 20s, but the rate rises slightly over 30, and then again over 40 (see Chapter 12).*
▶ *Chromosomal disorders are a more common finding in the eggs retrieved for IVF treatment (found in 25 per cent of the eggs of women under 35, and 47 per cent in those over 35).*
▶ *Incidences of Down's syndrome and other chromosomal disorders increase with age also.*

At its most basic, the longer you leave 'trying', the longer it's likely to take, on average, to conceive, and the less chance there is of a conception leading to a healthy pregnancy and birth.

This however all sounds far more gloomy than it is in reality, and statistics don't have to apply to you as an individual. Despite the figures, most women under 40 will conceive without a long delay, and will go on to have a normal pregnancy with a normal, healthy baby at the end of it. If they decide they want another baby, they'll probably be able to just as straightforwardly.

There are also individual men and women in their early 20s who experience fertility problems or problems with pregnancy and birth.

In short, it's a truism that if you want to get nature on your side, you'll start 'trying' sooner rather than later – which also gives you time to have any investigations or treatment if you do hit a challenge.

Of course, none of this takes into consideration the social issue of when you conceive. Older mothers and fathers may bring other positive qualities to the whole process of childbearing and parenting.

Case study – Rowena

We decided about six years ago – we got married, and during our honeymoon I decided to come off the pill. I assumed I'd be pregnant within months. Then nothing happened, no false alarms, nothing! A year later we both had initial fertility tests which were fine, then we forgot about it again. It was nearly four years since our wedding (I was now 34 and Adrian 44) and I suddenly thought: 'If I don't do something about this now, I probably won't ever have a baby'. That's when we really took it seriously and went for it.

Q&A

Is time running out at 37?

Q. I'm 37, and I've never been pregnant. I'm now with the first man I've met in a long time that I can imagine having children with. I'm scared that when we start trying, I'll find out I have a problem, and then it will be too late to get help...

A. A lot of women will identify with you. Science writer Vivienne Parry, writing in the *Guardian* about fertility clinics, says: 'One of the greatest design faults in humans is their lack of an external fertility indicator. When you're 38, and the bloke has finally appeared on your horizon, the idea of waiting for two years to see if you can make babies is not an option, given that IVF success after 40 has begun a freefall descent. Even six months of fruitless bonking at this age is enough to send couples rushing headlong to infertility clinics, though conception might have happened by itself in time.'

However, while what Parry says is true and you can't tell by looking if either of you is fertile, if you're still having regular periods and you're both in good health, there's no reason to think you won't be able to conceive. You might want to tip the odds in your favour though, by making sure you have sex at the time of ovulation, and using some of the other tips in Chapter 4. At 37, there's no reason to panic, but you might as well make all the right moves!

Insight

Don't let statistics depress you. A lot of conclusions from research only emerge when hundreds or thousands of cases are studied. Individual experience can't be predicted very well.

Men and fertility

The statistics show that men's fertility (the ability to reproduce) starts to decrease after the age of 35, and their fecundity (the actual rate of reproduction) after the age of 40, especially if their partner is of a similar age or older. In addition, there is evidence of sperm quality decreasing with age.

The biggest recent study of today's fathers, based on data from the Danish Fertility Database which has information on 70,000 couples and their first child, shows that older men have a higher risk of fathering a child with a disability. It's been known for some time that sperm acquire mutations as they age, and that there's a drop in male fertility as men get older. Now, epidemiologists find that the Danish data shows that men over 50 are more than four times more likely to have a child with Down's syndrome, and children with different types of limb defects. There's also evidence that older fathers are associated with a higher rate of a number of disorders in their offspring. A recent epidemiological study showed that the offspring of older fathers have reduced fertility and an increased risk of birth defects, some cancers, and schizophrenia (Bray, Gunnell, Davey-Smith 2006). These effects are only measurable with an overview of very large populations. As one study puts it:

> *Even if the genetic risk for progeny from older fathers is slightly increased, the risk to the individual is low.*
>
> *Reproductive functions of the ageing male*, Kuhnert B, Nieschlag E.
> Hum Reprod Update, 2004 Jul–Aug; 10(4): 327–39.

It's worth bearing in mind that you're far more likely to father a child easily and with no problems in the timing and in the subsequent pregnancy than not, whatever your age.

In the press – Do older men have less intelligent children?

New research suggesting that the age of your father influences your IQ – the older he was when you were born, the worse you are likely to fare when tested – is the latest addition to growing evidence that it is not just maternal age that matters when it comes to starting a family. [...] Children born to men aged over 35 are more likely to have a cleft lip or palate, congenital heart defects, and to develop some

Bypassing nature and planning ahead

So maybe the time isn't right for you now – but you can imagine some future date when circumstances will improve, or major obligations are behind you, allowing you to conceive and become pregnant at a more appropriate time. For a few people, men and women, safeguarding potential fertility becomes a decision they take as a result of serious illness; these decisions can be fraught with ethical problems at some later stage, as news items of legal actions and legislation show.

Currently, there's no immediate possibility of the option of cryopreservation – storage of tissue by freezing – being anything like a reliable or routine way of 'deferring' fertility. Legal issues about 'ownership' of embryos, eggs and sperm may mean they cannot be used by anyone if circumstances – and relationships – change at some future point.

FREEZING EMBRYOS

This almost always happens alongside ongoing fertility treatment, principally IVF or ICSI (Intra Cytoplasmic Sperm Injection). Good quality 'spare' embryos are frozen and kept in storage for a defined period (this changes with legislation – see Chapter 13 for more information). If you wish to become pregnant again at a later stage, one or more embryos will be thawed and placed in the uterus. If one of you changes your mind, the embryos cannot continue to be stored and will be destroyed. At present, the law in the UK says you must actively give your consent at intervals for continued storage.

There are similar issues if the eggs or the sperm don't come from you or your partner, and are donated ('donor gametes' is the technical term for donated eggs and sperm). Donors need to consent to storage and can withdraw their permission at any stage.

The science of embryo freezing is fairly well established, but pregnancy is rather less likely with a thawed embryo than with a fresh one. You should ask your clinic for the details of their success rate: while there seems to be no reason at present to think babies resulting from stored embryos are any different from other babies, informing yourself of the research into long-term outcomes makes sense. One clinic in 2007 estimated that successful transfer rates are between 20 and 25 per cent. 'Take home baby' rates are likely to be rather lower.

(Some people store embryos because they wish to avoid the risk of passing on an inherited condition, and storage allows embryos to be screened before implantation – none of this is the subject of this book, and will need to be researched elsewhere if it is of interest to you.)

In the press – Woman loses battle to use frozen embryos created with her ex-fiancé

Would-be mother left distraught by judgement

Former partner says he fought for 'basic principle'

A woman left infertile by cancer treatment lost her five-year battle yesterday for the right to use the frozen embryos that she created with her former partner.

Natallie Evans, 35, took her case through the UK courts and on to the European Court of Human Rights in Strasbourg after her former fiancé, Howard Johnston, withdrew his consent for her to try to conceive with the embryos.

But yesterday she reached the end of the road when the 17-judge grand chamber in Strasbourg ruled against her by 13–4.

Ms Evans, who is now with a new partner, had six eggs fertilized with Mr Johnston's sperm during IVF treatment in 2001, shortly before undergoing treatment for ovarian cancer that left her infertile.

Guardian, 11 April 2007

In the press – Born a record 13 years after embryo was frozen

The child could have been born in 1993 but its first experience of the world came 13 years later, or nine months after an embryo was pulled out of the freezer at a Spanish fertility clinic.

The clinic in Barcelona is claiming the world record for having brought about the birth of what could be termed the world's oldest baby...

... The fertilized egg was one of six created by the genetic parents, three of which were used in the original treatment. The three others were put up for adoption, and at least one was accepted by the new couple.

Guardian, 4 November 2006

FREEZING EGGS

This is considered to have fewer problems with 'ownership' than embryo storage – given that only one party is involved – and it's possible that science will make strides to improve the outcomes of the procedure which involves eggs being collected after the ovaries are stimulated by hormone injection, and selected ones then being frozen and stored.

A lecture, 'Deferring Motherhood', given by the University of Sheffield's Professor William Ledger in March 2007 at the Royal College of Obstetricians and Gynaecologists addressed the question. 'Why not freeze eggs at age 25 and use them at age 45?' The fertilization procedure is carried out post-thaw with ICSI, and it appears that approximately 70 per cent fertilize – though very few of these will result in a pregnancy, or a successful birth.

There is work being done to investigate freezing ovarian tissue, and then re-grafting it, to 'restart' ovulation after treatment for cancer. There are a handful of case studies which show this can be successful, resulting in a normal pregnancy and birth. At present this is cutting edge technology, but with advances being made all the time, it may prove to be useful.

In the press – Putting motherhood on ice

Egg-freezing has become more widespread over the past five years as techniques for egg-freezing have improved. Melbourne IVF, which has done 32 'social' egg freezes in the past decade, has now had two babies born from such eggs.

The Queensland Fertility Group has reported seven successful pregnancies from frozen eggs. Two of the pregnancies, one resulting in twins, were the result of social freezing.

According to Melbourne IVF fertility specialist Dr Kate Stern, new techniques have improved the survival rate of thawed eggs from one in five to six in ten.

'Now with ten eggs, we would expect six to survive, and ultimately make three embryos. Even with non-frozen eggs, only 50 per cent will fertilise,' Dr Stern said.

Melbourne Age, 31 May 2009

Insight

Be realistic: egg and embryo freezing is not a good bet for most women wanting to become pregnant. The technology is still too new and may never present a reliable alternative.

STORING SPERM

The technology of storing sperm is well established, and donor sperm has been used for many years. Sperm can be stored in a frozen state indefinitely before thawing – certainly for decades – but in the UK there is a legal time limit for the storage of genetic material, currently ten years. For deferring or prolonging fertility, sperm can be stored prior to treatment that might render the man infertile, or it can be stored to fertilize eggs at some later date, as part of a series of attempts at IVF or ICSI. Some men opt to freeze sperm before vasectomy – this allows a window of opportunity in the future, if he changes his mind about further children (perhaps if he has a new partner).

Current UK regulations specify the length of time sperm can be stored. Sperm are pretty resilient, and while a few do not survive the freezing process, the ones that do are undamaged.

In the press – Girl born a record 22 years after father's sperm is frozen

A former leukaemia patient who had his sperm frozen as a teenager has fathered a baby after doctors successfully thawed his sample a record 22 years later.

Chris Biblis was 16 when doctors told him that he needed radiotherapy that would leave him sterile and recommended before going ahead with the life-saving treatment that they put a sample of his sperm into cryogenic storage for future use.

Now aged 38, he is celebrating the birth of a healthy baby daughter, Stella, who was conceived after scientists injected a defrosted sperm into an egg from his wife, Melodie, and implanted it in her uterus.

The Times, 14 April 2009

THINGS TO REMEMBER

1 Late 'celebrity pregnancies' may be assisted by donors and not shared in the press.

2 The time may need to feel right, but don't leave it too long – there are risks.

3 It's your choice to judge when the timing is right for you.

4 Fear of childbirth can be treated.

5 Single motherhood is on the rise.

6 Raw figures on how much it costs to have a baby may be sensationalized.

7 Female fertility takes a sharp dip after the age of 35.

8 Male fertility is affected by age, but nowhere near as much as for women.

9 It's not realistic to rely on freezing eggs, sperm or embryos for future use.

2

How conception happens

In this chapter you will learn:
- *how the human body changes and prepares itself for conception*
- *how and when fertilization of the egg takes place*
- *what happens in the early days after the egg is fertilized.*

The process of conception is an amazingly complex one; there are so many aspects that need to work normally, but there is so much potential for them working less than well or not working at all. It's fair to say that while the bigger picture is pretty much understood, there's a great deal that's still to be fully appreciated about the smaller biochemical details. We don't yet know how to prevent some problems, while other problems are known and recognizable, but not yet fixable.

It's calculated that an averagely healthy, sexually active and fertile couple has a one in four chance of conceiving in any single contraception-free cycle. So, even when things are in full working order, in three months out of four, nothing happens.

Conception begins with sexual intercourse, but before then, separate 'preparations' have taken place in the man's body and the woman's body. For you to be fertile, and able to conceive, there are a lot of things that have to 'go right' with this preparation. Hormones need to be doing their job at the right time and in the right quantity, and there should be no barrier to the meeting of egg and sperm.

When conception fails to happen over a period of time, the problem lies in one (or more) of several areas:

▶ *problems with sexual intercourse itself – it may be not happening, or not happening at the right time, or the ejaculate is not getting into the vagina because of, for example, premature ejaculation*
▶ *problems with the production of eggs*
▶ *problems with the manufacture of sperm*
▶ *problems with sperm quality*
▶ *problems because of the way the uterus and/or fallopian tubes are functioning*
▶ *problems with the way the woman's body accepts the sperm.*

> **Insight**
> There are many complex processes that have to happen in both the male and the female halves of a couple before the egg gets anywhere near the sperm... Conception is an amazing phenomenon.

Getting ready... in the woman

It's amazing to think, but a baby girl at just seven months gestation, two months before birth, has the very beginnings of her own future pregnancies, sitting there, in each of her two ovaries.

Something like 7 million primordial follicles are present at that time. They each consist of a primary oocyte (egg) and a layer of cells. From that time on, the primordial follicles start to decrease in number, and they're already down to 2 million at birth. Throughout childhood and adulthood, the 'attrition rate' continues; at menarche, the start of menstruation, they number about 300,000, and by the time of the menopause at age about 50, there may be about 1,000 left.

Only about two in every 1,000 primordial follicles actually become eggs, and an even tinier proportion ever become fertilized. The development of the eggs stop until the female reaches puberty, which is when the body begins the production and release of mature eggs – 'ova', singular 'ovum' – at menarche (pronounced 'men-ar-kay'). This is the time when menstrual periods begin, which usually happens at some point between the ages of ten and 15.

Eggs are not produced continuously (unlike sperm). Instead, they are produced at four-week intervals (roughly – it varies from person to person). These four weeks comprise the menstrual cycle, and the egg is released on or about day 14. Usually, only one egg is produced per cycle.

Hormones produced in the ovaries govern the timing of the menstrual cycle and its effects. It is hormones – oestrogen and progesterone – which are responsible for the development of other sexual characteristics, including breasts, and body and pubic hair.

Follicle stimulating hormone (FSH), produced by the pituitary gland at the base of the brain, works on the ovaries, and starts encouraging growth and development in each one of a bunch of 20 to 30 follicles on the surface of the ovary. The follicles ripen under this stimulation and the influence of oestrogen, nurturing the oocyte within. As the oocyte matures, it becomes the ovum.

Only one (usually) of the follicles gets to a fully mature stage as a result of being stimulated by luteinizing hormone, also from the pituitary. As the follicles ripen, they produce increasing amounts of the hormone oestrogen.

Oestrogen has two main effects:

▶ *it stimulates cervical mucus and*
▶ *it thickens the lining of the uterus.*

The most mature follicle is known as the graafian follicle, and at its 'ripest' point, it ruptures, and expels the ovum. This is ovulation. The ovum at this stage is about the size of the head on a pin, and its lifespan is about 12–24 hours. It heads for a space behind the uterus called the pouch of Douglas.

After ovulation, the empty follicle left behind starts to change. This is the 'luteal phase' of the menstrual cycle. The follicle forms a structure known as the corpus luteum (it just means 'yellow body', which is the colour of it). The corpus luteum, which exists for about 12–16 days, produces the hormone called progesterone, and the amount of progesterone increases as the days go by.

Progesterone's main effects are:

▶ *it thickens cervical mucus,*
▶ *it prevents the maturing of any other follicles – if a second ovulation happens, it takes place within no more than 24 hours (that's what happens with non-identical twins) and*
▶ *it causes the body's temperature to rise slightly.*

The next stage of the process is when one of the fallopian tubes picks up the ovum, using a sweeping-like motion of the tiny finger-like projections on its end. The egg is sucked into the tube itself, and wave-like motions transport the egg further on its journey, possibly to meet a sperm.

Remember!

Menstrual cycles are not always 28 days. Healthy women can have a much shorter, or a much longer cycle, and the normal range is between 21 and 35 days. Some women are healthy, but irregular.

Ovulation doesn't always happen 14 days before the period either. It can happen sooner or later than this.

Some menstrual cycles occur without any ovulation happening at all. This is normal for all women occasionally, and for some women frequently.

Insight
It's a good idea to keep a written note of your menstrual cycle – lots of women do it anyway, so they know when to expect a period. You can also watch for signs of ovulation and see if they happen about 14 days before your next period's due.

Getting ready... in the man

The male role in conception depends on him producing and then ejaculating sufficient numbers of effective sperm – with 'effective' meaning the sperm are motile (capable of swimming towards the egg). While only one sperm is actually needed at a time, normal fertility levels have that single sperm as one among several million in each ejaculation. Of these several million, around 100 survive the journey to the egg.

A man normally has two testicles or testes, each of which has a tube called the vas deferens which goes from the testis to the urethra. The urethra is the tube that takes urine from the bladder to the penis and which exits at the end of the penis. In addition, the prostate gland and seminal vesicles, which sit inside the body, between the bladder and the rectum, make secretions that form the seminal fluid, also known as semen.

The testes are outside the body, in the scrotum; they start their reproductive functioning at puberty, producing the hormone testosterone. It's testosterone that causes the other bodily changes at puberty, such as the growth of facial and body hair, and the deepening of the voice. In addition, the testes produce sperm, also called spermatozoa. This process is stimulated by follicle stimulating hormone and luteinizing hormone – the same hormones as in the female.

Sperm are produced continuously, at the rate of about 5,000 sperm cells every minute. They take about 70 days to fully mature. They are stored in the epididymus – a convoluted tube next to each testis – for about 12 days, where the maturing process continues. At ejaculation, sperm are propelled into the urethra, where they mix with semen from the seminal vesicles and the prostate gland. Semen nourishes and preserves the sperm, and supports their movement towards the egg. A typical ejaculation will be 98 per cent fluid and two per cent sperm.

Insight

Hardly any of the fluid ejaculated by a man consists of sperm – the vast majority of it is seminal fluid. There is no way you can tell if a man is fertile or not by gauging the amount of semen he ejaculates.

Getting together – when sperm meets egg

Because ovulation takes place only once per menstrual cycle (usually), there are only a few days each month when conception is likely to happen.

While the egg survives maybe 12–24 hours after ovulation, the 'window of opportunity' for conception is a little wider than that in practice, because healthy sperm can live for between two and three days. They can wait for ovulation to happen, just as the egg – which is present for up to a day – can wait for a sperm.

For most practical purposes, a woman's fertile period lasts about four days, and outside these times conception is highly unlikely. A second ovulation can (rarely) take place after the first, as we've seen, but no more than one day later.

TIMING CONCEPTION

Ovulation takes place 14 days before the onset of the next menstrual period. If conception happens, there is no period. A period is the shedding of the uterine lining, which has been preparing itself to nourish the fertilized egg. Your basal body temperature rises, and the mucus in your vagina becomes thinner and more slippery. If you're watching out for ovulation (see p. 48), you'll be aware of the signs it is about to happen, which show up in bodily changes.

A few women experience a sensation in the pelvis at the time of ovulation – it can be like a sharp pain or a dull ache and it can last up to a few hours. It's sometimes known as 'mittelschmerz', and it's thought to be related to muscular cramps in the uterus, but the exact cause is not known. It takes place just before ovulation.

So, having sexual intercourse at or near ovulation time brings the sperm into the vagina at a time when the cervical mucus, secreted into the vagina, is receptive. 'Fertile' mucus is alkaline, with higher levels than normal of water, salt and amino acids, which nourish the sperm. When the sperm enter the vagina, they're on their way to the uterus, and from there some reach the fallopian tubes.

If everything's been going normally, the egg is in one of the tubes, and somewhere in the first third of the tube's length, it meets a healthy, mature sperm. Fusion will then take place – egg and sperm join, and the sperm creates a chemical reaction which dissolves the outside of the ovum and allows the sperm to penetrate the egg. This penetration is fertilization.

The fertilized egg has the technical name of the 'zygote'. It consists of 23 pairs of chromosomes – genetic material. One chromosome in each pair comes from the male, and the other one of the pair comes from the female. Amazingly enough, in that very process, all the future baby's inherited characteristics are there – hair and eye colour, height, facial and body features and everything else you pass on. The sex of your baby depends on the type of sex chromosomes provided by the sperm. The ovum always supplies 22 chromosomes plus an X sex chromosome, whereas the sperm supplies 22 chromosomes plus an X or Y sex chromosome. Two X chromosomes will mean a female infant, and an X and a Y will mean a male.

Within a few days, the zygote reaches the uterus, wafted along the fallopian tube by the microscopically sized hairs on the inside of the tube. All the time it's travelling, it's developing and growing, by a process of cell division – four cells become eight, then 16 and so on. The cluster of cells is called a morula, which is the Latin term for 'mulberry', as that is what it resembles.

Once at the uterus, it starts to attach to the uterine wall, now ready and waiting and richly lined with blood. The cell cluster at this stage is termed a blastocyst, or an early embryo.

The uterine lining is known as the endometrium. Implantation – when the zygote embeds into the endometrium – takes place about six days after the egg is fertilized, and completes over the next few days. As implantation takes place, the embryo is developing a fluid-containing protective capsule. Around the embryo and its sac of fluid are two membranes, the inner amnion and the outer chorion. The chorion will become the placenta, and it starts to burrow into the uterus. This enables it to obtain nutrients from the mother's bloodstream. The chorion (later the placenta) also starts producing hormones which support the pregnancy – and it's these hormones which, it is thought, can contribute to pregnancy sickness. The presence of this hormone – human chorionic gonadotrophin or hCG – is what the pregnancy tests detect in your urine.

Two weeks after fertilization, or around the time you would have had a period, the embryo is embedded in the uterus. It's about one millimetre in size and, already, the first beginnings of the nervous system and the heart will be developing.

Insight

If you are pregnant, you might start to feel sickness and nausea even before you miss a period.

Remember!

Non-identical twins can be the same sex or different sexes. They result from two eggs, fertilized separately. Identical twins are the result of a spontaneous division of the zygote and are always the same sex.

X or Y?

People often ask: can I choose the sex of my baby? There have been theories in popular health books about this since the 1970s, and there are various methods of varying complexity that claim success.

Some people go through gender selection to avoid passing on an inherited condition that applies to one sex only (the most well known is haemophilia – a condition where the blood fails to clot properly – that affects boys only). The only way to be sure of having the 'right' sex is to go through IVF and replace only the 'right' embryo(s). This is not legal for anything other than medical reasons in several countries, including the UK. Aborting on the grounds of gender is not legal either. If you want to have a boy or a girl for purely social reasons, you're on your own. You can check out the internet for a number of theories, and see how bothered you are to put them into practice. They are all based on trying to create an environment that favours the 'Y' chromosome of the sperm.

- **Diet.** *There are many do's and don'ts with regard to diet. The main difference in the most common theories is that the 'boy' diet is high in salt, and has no milk, while the opposite is the case for the 'girl' diet. Check you're not changing your diet so drastically that it becomes unhealthy (high salt is not a good idea long term).*
- **Timing.** *For a boy, have sex as close as you can to the time of ovulation, within 24 hours either way. For a girl, don't get any closer than 48 hours.*
- **pH.** *Changing the pH (acidity) of the vagina by douching the vagina before intercourse. The long-standing Shettles method (from Dr Landrum B. Shettles, who wrote about it) details how water and vinegar (acid) should be used for a girl, and water and baking soda for a boy (get the book – still in print – for further instructions, and for how it combines with timing).*

The truth is that there is no truly substantiated way of tipping the scales one way or the other.

Clinics have been reported in newspapers as offering a service by which the sperm is put into a centrifuge and spun, which is supposed to separate X chromosome sperm from Y chromosome sperm, and the 'right' sperm are then placed in the vagina at the right time. The method is known as 'gradient sorting', and it does not have a very high success rate.

The other method of separating sperm is called flow cytometry – *New Scientist*, 12 November 2003, describes it thus:

> *This involves adding a fluorescent dye to a sperm sample which stains genetic material. Because sperm carrying an X chromosome have more DNA than Y-bearing sperm, they attract more dye.*

There are concerns about the effect of the dye on the sperm, however, and this method is not available in the UK, even when gender selection is supported with a medical reason.

Think about why you want a boy or a girl – what does it say about you if it becomes very important to have the 'right' sex, without putting health and happiness first? What if the baby you get is the 'wrong' sex? Will you be disappointed? Would this somehow transmit to your baby as he or she grows? All food for thought!

In the press – It's a boy! The science of sex selection

In what they claim is the first scientific evidence that diet influences infant gender, researchers at the Universities of Exeter and Oxford have found that women who consume more calories around the time of conception, and, in particular, eat more bananas, are more likely to have sons. At the same time, those who skip breakfast (and breakfast seems to be key) are more likely to have daughters.

Independent, 24 April 2008

Insight

There's no sure way to select the sex of your baby, so it's best not to have strong hopes one way or the other.

Q&A

Should I really go teetotal?

Q. I'm not a heavy drinker, but at weekends, I share a bottle of wine or two with my partner, and if we go out with friends, I have a couple of drinks. I hear different things about the wisdom of having alcohol in any quantity

(Contd)

at all – I would like to become pregnant soon, but what if it takes a while? I don't really want people to know we're trying for a baby either – stopping drinking draws attention to it, and invites comment.

A. The research into alcohol and pregnancy, and alcohol and fertility, is pretty consistent, in that it shows there is an effect. But the lower 'safe limit' is not consistent. Obviously, if you don't drink any alcohol at all, you're sure to be safe from any effects, as there's no research showing any benefit to alcohol, but it's really not crystal clear that occasional drinking tips the balance into 'risky behaviour', or that it makes a measurable difference to your chances of conception if everything else is normal.

There are studies of large numbers of women that do show both of these things, and you might want to check these out. Some studies suggest that infertile or sub-fertile women should abstain from all alcohol, but findings are inconclusive.

It's understandable you want to keep your conception journey private, and to avoid inviting comment. If this is a difficult issue for you, then why not compromise? If you do decide to cut down on your alcohol consumption, you could avoid drinking at home and gradually reduce the amount you drink in public – no one will notice if you mix your wine with soda, or simply slow your intake down when you're with other people.

THINGS TO REMEMBER

1 *An averagely healthy, sexually active and fertile couple has a one in four chance of conceiving in any single contraception-free cycle.*

2 *When conception fails to happen over a period of time, the problem may lie in one or more of several areas.*

3 *A baby girl, two months before birth, already has the very beginnings of her own future pregnancies in her ovaries.*

4 *From 7 million oocytes before birth, there are 1,000 left at age 50.*

5 *Eggs are produced at roughly four-week intervals, one per menstrual cycle.*

6 *The lifespan of an egg is about 12 to 24 hours.*

7 *Healthy women can have a much shorter, or a much longer cycle than 28 days – the normal range is between 21 and 35 days.*

8 *Ovulation usually happens 14 days before the next period is due.*

9 *Of several million sperm in the ejaculate, about 100 get anywhere near the egg.*

10 *The window of opportunity for conception is a few days only, every four weeks.*

3

....

Very early pregnancy – from embryo to foetus

In this chapter you will learn:
- *about body changes during the first weeks of pregnancy*
- *how the embryo matures in these first weeks*
- *about the early assessment tests available.*

Early developments

Despite the lack of anything to see in these very early weeks, there's a great deal of physiological work going on 'underneath'.

Some of the activity can affect the way you feel physically and emotionally – that's discussed in greater detail in Chapter 10.

In this chapter, we'll take a look at the unseen changes that take place after implantation – the time when the embryo embeds in the endometrium (the lining on the uterus wall), and when the chorion starts to receive nourishment from the mother's blood to supply the embryo.

The chorion is the beginning of the placenta, which remains to do its job of feeding the embryo (later, foetus – the embryo 'officially' becomes a foetus at the eighth week of pregnancy) until the very moment the umbilical cord is cut after birth. The foetal blood circulation starts to develop during this time – the mother's circulation and the foetus' circulation will always remain separate from each other. Throughout pregnancy, nutrients and oxygen from the maternal blood go into the placenta, and from there move into the foetus, without the two blood systems combining at any one point.

At this point, the embryo is encased in the amniotic sac. The sac is made up of two very thin, transparent membranes. The inner membrane is known as the amnion. This is filled with amniotic fluid in which the foetus is held – a wet environment which will persist all the way through pregnancy, until birth.

The major organs start to appear in a very basic form during the first eight weeks of pregnancy. 'Limb buds' – small buds that will become arms and legs – form, and the foetal heart starts beating. The central nervous system is also there, in a primitive form.

There are the very beginnings of facial features, too, by week six of the pregnancy. Small folds of skin on each side of the head will become the ears, and indentations on the face will become the mouth and nostrils. An ultrasound scan is capable of identifying the foetus at this stage, and a heartbeat can sometimes be detected.

In most cases, a scan would not be used unless there was some reason to suspect an ectopic pregnancy – a pregnancy that's developing outside the uterus, usually in the fallopian tube.

By the eighth week of pregnancy (six weeks after fertilization), the embryo is 1–2 centimetres in length. Measurements are taken from the crown to the rump (this is called the crown-rump length, or the CRL).

Insight

Early scans are normally only offered for specific medical reasons. Your routine scan checks for multiple pregnancy, confirms your dates, and confirms the foetus is growing normally. You may have an early scan if you have had IVF.

Hormones

When implantation happens, the embryo begins to make hormones, principally hCG (human chorionic gonadotrophin), which reaches the maternal bloodstream. It is hCG that's detected in your urine when you come to take a pregnancy test (see Chapter 2).

In addition, the production of hCG has the important role of stimulating the continued production of hormones by the corpus luteum (the empty follicle where the egg came from). If you were not pregnant, the corpus luteum would cease to function, and progesterone levels would drop. But under the influence of hCG, the production of hormones progesterone and oestrogen continues throughout the pregnancy.

This is gradually taken over by the placenta, as it develops during the first trimester (the first three months of pregnancy). Progesterone stops menstruation and prevents any further ovulation; oestrogen stimulates growth in the embryo. Progesterone also maintains the health of the mother and the embryo, and sets in motion changes in the breast tissue (so there will be milk storage and milk production when the baby is born) and works on strengthening the uterus and the cervix.

The right levels of hormones are so crucial to these early pregnancy days that research is currently underway to investigate ways of assessing low hormone levels in repeated early miscarriage. Supporting early pregnancy by giving the expectant mother extra hormones to boost her own production may turn out to be a treatment for recurrent miscarriage.

Insight

The pregnancy is sustained by the right level of hormones, marshalling the right biochemical environment for the embryo to grow, and ensuring the uterus is a safe place.

Screening tests

If you're healthy and you have no reason to expect anything but a normal pregnancy, any screening tests to check on the health and development of your baby would not be done until much later – the first antenatal ultrasound scan is not usually offered until about 12 weeks, and routine blood samples are not taken until your 'booking' appointment, which is normally no earlier than 10 weeks or so. (It's called 'booking' as the maternity unit is normally notified of your pregnancy at that time – but it doesn't mean you can't change the place you have your baby at some future date).

However, some tests may be offered sooner, if there's a clinical reason for them.

You may have a very early ultrasound scan at six to eight weeks if:

- ▶ *you've experienced bleeding*
- ▶ *there's some concern about whether you have an ectopic pregnancy (see pp. 39 and 155)*
- ▶ *it's not certain if you're still pregnant.*

Very early scans may be done vaginally – with a probe that enters the vagina, rather than the more usual method of using a sensor that moves over the abdomen.

It's possible to have a 'sex selection' test very early and, controversially, some private services are offering these tests (at a price) as early as six weeks, claiming a 99 per cent accuracy rate. A drop of the mother's blood is tested by looking for foetal DNA. If the 'Y' chromosome is present, the prediction is for a boy.

These tests are not brand new, and they have been used in trials to check for gender-specific conditions, such as Duchenne muscular dystrophy, which affects boys only.

Current medical and ethical opinion is against testing solely for gender – as opposed to finding out as a side-effect of an ultrasound scan at 20 or so weeks – as it's thought it could increase the chances of a female foetus being aborted. However, according to the manufacturers, this has not happened when the test has been on sale in the United States.

Selecting for sex on medical grounds is more usually done after IVF, when embryos are tested, and an embryo of one gender and not the other is selected to be put into the uterus.

THINGS TO REMEMBER

1 *Implantation is the time when the embryo embeds in the endometrium (the lining on the uterus wall).*

2 *The mother's blood circulation and the foetus' circulation always remain separate from each other.*

3 *Throughout pregnancy, nutrients and oxygen from the maternal blood go into the placenta, and from there move into the foetus.*

4 *The major organs start to appear in a very basic form during the first eight weeks of pregnancy.*

5 *'Limb buds' – small buds that will become arms and legs – form from eight weeks.*

6 *The embryo makes the hormone hCG, which is detected by a pregnancy test in your urine.*

7 *The hormone progesterone stops menstruation and prevents any further ovulation once an egg has been fertilized.*

8 *The first routine antenatal ultrasound scan is offered at about 12 weeks.*

9 *By the eighth week of pregnancy (six weeks after fertilization), the embryo is 1–2 centimetres in length.*

10 *Research is investigating the role of low hormone levels in repeated early miscarriage.*

4

Fertility awareness –
get biology on your side

In this chapter you will learn:
- *how to become aware of your fertility*
- *how to detect signs and symptoms to increase your chances of conception*
- *about monitors and kits as an additional way of checking your fertility.*

Contraception works in three basic ways:

▶ *it presents a physical barrier to stop sperm and egg getting together, or*
▶ *it changes the hormonal profile so the body becomes 'hostile' to conception, or*
▶ *it restricts sexual intercourse to the times when pregnancy is least likely.*

There are a number of 'natural' contraceptive methods that use fertility awareness; it's perfectly feasible to use the same principles in the opposite way, to make it more likely that you will conceive. You can use all of them, some of them or pick the one method that seems easiest to you. All of them involve increasing the chances you 'hit' ovulation – which as we saw in Chapter 2 is the release of the egg – which survives in a fertilizable state for between 12 and 24 hours only.

That doesn't mean you only have one day maximum to become pregnant each month – sperm survive and remain capable of fertilizing the egg for two to three days (sometimes even seven days), and can be present before the egg is released. This extends the window of opportunity, though not by much.

Insight

Because sperm survive after ejaculation, a woman is fertile for longer than the time the egg remains available – sperm can be there 'waiting' for an egg for a few days.

Frequent enough sex

If you go a long time without having sexual intercourse, you may be missing some or even all your chances to conceive in any given cycle.

The classic, almost clichéd story is the one where a couple go to their doctor having tried to conceive for a year, and it emerges that the man is a long distance lorry driver who is away from home one week in every four – and guess which week? A change of schedule in that situation means that the 'away week' coincides with a week other than the one that falls in the middle of his partner's menstrual cycle.

It's logical that sex a week apart, or even more than three or four days apart, may not hit the right time for a while (of course, it depends on what days the gaps fall, but if you're not counting out your cycle, you won't know this).

Insight

There are many myths about becoming pregnant, but most of them don't check out well. Finding out when you ovulate and scheduling sex to hit the right time is the soundest method.

Is it possible for sex to become too frequent? What about the quantity of sperm available? If a man has sex or masturbates more often than he can 'replace' his sperm, might this affect his fertility? It seems not, or at least the studies that have looked at the variation in sperm count between men indicate that frequency of ejaculation only accounts for a very small variation in amount. Sperm numbers do vary – they seem to go up and down within the individual, and there's a falling off with age too. However, frequent intercourse is not something to avoid – or at least there's no substantial evidence that says it will make any difference if you avoid it.

> **Insight**
> Deliberately withholding sperm by avoiding ejaculation for a couple of days does not make a man more fertile.

It might be something to ask about if the man in a partnership is known to be less than normally fertile – 'saving up' sperm for a couple of days as well as timing sex may be worth a try, though there's no sound evidence that this has any measurable impact on conception. More frequent ejaculations – either as a result of sex or masturbation – reduces the concentration of sperm, but has no effect on their shape or movement (*Fertility and Sterility*, August 2004). From the point of view of chances to conceive, there seems to be no point in having sex more often than every two days – but of course you can have it more often if you want!

Case study – Marion

When we decided to go for it, we did really work on it, and agreed not to let more than three or four days pass without sex. It worked a charm in the first month of trying.

SCHEDULING SEX

One step more specific than just deciding to have sex often enough is to deliberately schedule it, so it coincides with the time you're most likely to ovulate. This involves counting days to work out your most fertile time.

For most women on a regular menstrual cycle, this isn't difficult, as it's most likely to be 14 days before your next period is due, or to extend the window, 17–13 days before, or days 11, 12, 13, 14 and 15 of your cycle. The first day of your period counts as day 1. On day 13–14, you'll probably ovulate. The egg will then survive until day 14–15. However, sperm can 'hang around' for 2–3 days or even longer, surviving up to five or even seven days, so intercourse on days 9, 10 and/or 11 might just allow a sperm to remain until ovulation happens.

The most fertile time for you both is likely to be when egg and sperm are 'fresh' and raring to go – so true scheduling will mean making sure you have sex on day 13, and for good measure, on both days either side of that, too.

Some women make a note in their diary of these times to save the mental arithmetic each month. Bear in mind that many women don't ovulate at the 'usual' time, so you may decide to be even more specific than dating your cycle to find out your fertile days.

Remember!

Your cycle may not be perfectly regular each month, so regular intercourse from day 9 of your cycle to day 17 will make the most of any window of opportunity.

Women with a long menstrual cycle (more than 28 days) ovulate later in their cycle than women with a short menstrual cycle (less than 28 days) but it can still happen as early as day 8, or as late as day 16 or 17.

Case study – Sue

I'd been on the pill for some years, then came off intending to try and get pregnant in a year or so – that was the plan, anyway.

(Contd)

My best friend, who's a nurse, told me she'd been trying to conceive for many months, with no luck. Then one day she overheard a gynaecologist telling a patient the 'recipe' for becoming pregnant. She excitedly told me the recipe and determined that she would try it. She did and she got pregnant the next month.

I was so excited and delighted at her success that I threw caution to the wind and tried it myself the following month. Bingo! It was really nice that we were pregnant together.

Sadly, I then miscarried at nine weeks. I waited for my next period and we tried again. I became pregnant again straight away, and my baby and my friend's baby were born four months apart.

The recipe was very simple – make love after your period has ended, then abstain until 14 days before you expect your next period, make love then and once more – once more only – 48 hours later. That's it! It's easy peasy. Apparently, it's to do with mature sperm being more able to fertilize an egg, because they're better at penetrating it.

I've since told the 'recipe' to many women, and I know of many babies born as a result. Most people express surprise that making love more frequently actually lessens your chance of conceiving.

Insight

Scheduling sex can be stressful for both of you and your partner. Talk about your feelings and be open about feeling pressured; you could try a month off, and start being spontaneous once more.

Pinpointing ovulation

If you want to be more sure of hitting the right time, there are other symptoms to look for that help you decide on the day.

Hormonal effects, principally by the hormone progesterone secreted from the corpus luteum after ovulation, cause your body to warm up very slightly once ovulation has happened. The difference in temperature is 0.2 of a degree centigrade, and it shows up on waking in the morning. This is known as your basal body temperature or BBT. This slightly elevated temperature remains until your next period.

Remember!

It's after ovulation that this happens – so you can't use temperature changes to say ovulation is about to happen.

You can track your BBT with a special fertility thermometer. You can buy a standard old-style mercury thermometer from a chemist or over the internet, with large divisions to make reading easier, or for only a small amount more, the easy-to-use digital version. Some thermometers store previous readings, which will help you.

Here's how to take your BBT:

1 *Starting on the first day of your period, before you get up, eat or drink anything, take your temperature in the usual way, placing the thermometer in your mouth.*
2 *Repeat this every morning at approximately the same time. Record your findings on a graph (you can download this from the internet – graphs for this are available on many sites).*
3 *Watch for the slight rise in temperature, from about day 13–14 of your cycle. It shows you have ovulated.*

Insight

Buy a made-for-the-purpose fertility thermometer rather than trying to squint at the scale on a normal one.

If you want to be more accurate about your time of ovulation, you can look for different symptoms of it. The type and texture of your cervical secretions – the mucus in your vagina – changes at different points of your cycle. Getting to be familiar with these changes takes practice, and you can become quite skilled at noticing even quite small differences. You can examine your secretions by looking at traces on your underwear, by wiping yourself with toilet paper and seeing what results, and by inserting and then removing a finger and testing the mucus on your finger.

The pattern to watch for is as follows:

▶ *When your period ends, you will probably be fairly 'dry' and you may not see or feel very much at all.*
▶ *In response to the increasing amount of oestrogen in your body, your cervix starts to produce more mucus, which at first is sticky, and may be white or creamy in colour.*
▶ *After a few days of this, your mucus changes to become thinner and slippery, and clear in colour. The usual comparison is to raw egg white – it has that stretchy quality, too, and you may be able to produce a string of it between finger and thumb. When you notice this fertile mucus, you're at the start of the most fertile time of your cycle.*

It's normal for the amount of secretion to vary from month to month, or for you to notice no difference occasionally. You can keep a record of your observations, with dates and times, to help you see a pattern emerging.

Insight

After a month or two of checking your cervical mucus, you'll become very skilled at noticing even small changes.

Case study – Rowena

I used a temperature-monitoring device that records your waking temperature every morning and works out when you're about to ovulate. I have a short cycle (27 days), and had always assumed I ovulated in the middle of the month – usual info is that it's 14 days before the first day of the period. It turned out that I ovulated at day 18. I conceived on the third month of using it, so it was money well spent. Amazing to think it only took three months of being systematic, after four years of trying! It's really easy to use, and I use it now for natural contraception.

OTHER SIGNS OF OVULATION

The position of your cervix changes during your cycle, and if you feel it, it changes its texture. These changes begin about six days before ovulation, and the cervix then reverts back to its previous condition one or two days afterwards, indicating the end of your fertile time.

Here's what you will notice, if you insert a finger into your vagina and touch your cervix.

▶ *Before the changes begin, your cervix will feel comparatively low in the vagina, easily reached by a finger tip; the surface of the cervix is firm, and it feels a bit like touching the end of your nose; the surface feels dryish; the os – the opening to the cervix which feels like a little dimple – is closed.*
▶ *As the changes start, your cervix feels raised, and your finger will need to go in a little further to touch it; the surface feels softer; it's wetter because of the mucus being produced; the os feels open.*

A tip is to always feel for the cervix when you're standing or squatting in the same position, as changes in the way you stand or sit can alter the way you feel it. You don't need to be rough in any way, as the changes are easily detectable with gentle touching. It only takes a few seconds to check things out, when you are practised.

Again, you can record these observations on a chart, with dates and times.

LESS CLEAR SIGNS

It's reasonably easy to record aspects of your body you can measure and track over time, but less easy to be aware of changes in mood or sex drive. Some women are very sensitive to these differences, and if they happen regularly enough around the same time, then they're probably fairly trustworthy as a sign of ovulation.

Case study – Prya

As soon as we decided the time was 'now', I bought an ovulation kit so we could make sure of trying to conceive at the right time. We worked it all out very carefully. We left it until after Christmas and the New Year, so I could have a drink without worrying if I was already pregnant. We were successful the second month.

Maybe you feel a greater (or lesser) sex drive. Perhaps you're aware of a change of mood. Some women find their breasts are more sensitive around the time of ovulation. There's also the possibility of actually feeling ovulation as a short-lived ache or pain (see p. 31).

Tracking your cycle with a kit

There are a number of commercially packed kits to help you monitor your menstrual cycle, all based on the symptoms and changes your body goes through. They're called ovulation predictor kits, and they're widely available in chemists and over the internet.

The 'invisible' signs of ovulation are the rise in certain hormones, which show up in the symptoms detailed on previous pages; ovulation predictor kits are able to test for these hormones, and by noting the different results, you can accurately see when you've hit your fertile time.

Ovulation predictor kits (OPKs) check for the presence of luteinizing hormone or LH, in the urine. Different brands have slightly different modes of action, so what follows here is no more than a generalization.

LH is present in a woman's body throughout the menstrual cycle, but just before ovulation there's a marked and usually fairly sudden rise in production, which can be detected in bodily fluids. With a sensitive kit, the beginning of this rise can be detected 36 hours before ovulation.

Kits provide you with throw-away, one-use-only sticks ('pee sticks') which you either urinate onto, mid-stream, or dip into some collected urine. Alternatively, you can use strips. You would normally be advised to test at some time beyond mid-morning or in the afternoon – this is because the LH surge happens in the morning, and it will take a few hours to be present in your urine.

Impregnated in the stick/strip is a membrane with anti-LH antibodies in it, which detect the amount of LH present in the urine. You can see if the test is 'positive' or 'negative' by the presence of a colour band which changes if sufficient LH is present. You compare the intensity of colour with the control band on the same strip/stick. It normally takes 3–5 minutes for this reaction to take place.

Other brands show a digital display of positive or negative, which might be easier to understand – it's up to you. Some women become experts in the different types of OPKs – it's worth looking on internet forums to keep up with consumer reports and new brands. It's also worth noting that the LH surge does not guarantee ovulation – you may see a surge, but not release an egg.

USING A SALIVA-BASED TEST

You can now buy a home-use ovulation microscope that tests your saliva for 'ferning' – the characteristic crystalline pattern formed by a sample of dried saliva in the days leading up to ovulation. The microscope is tiny – no bigger than a lipstick case – and easy to use. Hormone and salt changes in the body are reflected in the saliva, and with an accuracy of about 98 per cent, peering through the little lens is a quick way to check on your most fertile days. Ask in chemists or look on the internet for suppliers.

Case study – Ruth

After two boys, I read up on the information about using timing to have a girl. When I actually became pregnant though, it wasn't planned... The 'accident' just so happened at a time my findings had suggested a girl would be more likely. And it proved to be true!

You normally need to start testing before you expect ovulation to happen, and that will depend on the length of your cycle (starting earlier with a short cycle). Again, it's all in the instructions that come with your pack of sticks or strips. It can take time to find the brand and the method you like and can interpret easily, so if you want to go with this way of checking the timing of your fertility, experimenting with different types is a good idea.

FERTILITY MONITORS

Monitors are hand-held devices to interpret your test sticks – they are quite recent developments. They can be programmed with information on the time and length of your cycle, and can also detect the presence of oestrogen as well as LH from the sticks. A high oestrogen level will stimulate the rise in LH, which as we've seen, comes just before ovulation.

The digital display on the device reads the stick for you, and distinguishes between high, low and peak fertility. If you have intercourse on the day of peak fertility, you maximize your chances of becoming pregnant.

Signs of ovulation – and no ovulation

Not all cycles release an egg. Nature is not 100 per cent perfect – you can have some signs of ovulation, which then cease, because for some reason it doesn't happen. With a monitor, this can sometimes be detected when the 'high' fertility does not become 'peak'; or you may see a change in mucus, but it passes very quickly.

If you're investigated for fertility problems, checking out your ovulation 'performance' would be one of the assessments you'd be offered, but one egg-free cycle would not mean you were not ovulating at all.

In the press – Hormone offers promise as fertility treatment

New research suggests the hormone kisspeptin shows promise as a potential new treatment for infertility. [...] Scientists led by Dr Waljit Dhillo from Imperial College London, have shown that giving kisspeptin to women with infertility can activate the release of sex hormones which control the menstrual cycle. This research could lead to a new fertility therapy for women with low sex hormone levels.

Kisspeptin is a product of the KISS-1 gene and is a key regulator of reproductive function. Animals and humans lacking kisspeptin function do not go through puberty and remain sexually immature. In a previous study, Dr Waljit Dhillo and colleagues showed that kisspeptin treatment leads to the production of sex hormones in fertile women; they have now extended their research to look at the effects of kisspeptin in women whose periods have stopped due to a hormone imbalance.

Society for Endocrinology, press release, 17 March 2009

Use of the pill

Q. I've been using the contraceptive pill for more than seven years now, and I stopped to become pregnant. I haven't yet had a period, but I know I haven't conceived. Has the pill affected my fertility?

A. Almost certainly not – there have been a number of studies looking at this, and it's seen that there is no long-term difference in fertility between women who have used oral contraception and those that haven't. There is a variable individual response in the first months after you come off the pill – it may take you a few cycles to resume a regular pattern, or you may immediately establish one, which may (or may not) be the same as the pattern you had before.

If you continue not to have periods for, say, six months and you know you're not pregnant, it would be reasonable to speak to your doctor about it. But it's highly likely all is well.

Are problems inherited?

Q. My maternal grandmother had one child only, when she was 39. It's never been discussed, but they had been married about ten years, and I don't think they deliberately tried to avoid pregnancy. My mother had me at 43, after years of trying to have babies, and I'm an only child as well. Is difficulty having children hereditary? Am I likely to have problems, too?

A. Most of the issues associated with fertility problems are not hereditary, and actually, the medical, surgical and pharmaceutical treatments now available would not have been a possibility for your mother or your grandmother. There's some evidence that early menopause runs in families, but with pregnancies at 39 and 43, clearly that didn't apply to your mother and grandmother.

Other ways to test at home

Home assessments can be done for male and female fertility, and it's worthwhile checking the internet for updates on methods and kits available, and comparing prices, too.

For women, you can go beyond checking LH and now monitor your urine for follicle stimulating hormone (FSH). You don't test for it at the same time as checking for LH. Instead, you check for FSH near the beginning of your cycle, on day three.

FSH testing is based on the knowledge of how fertility declines with age. We have already seen that infant females have their quota of eggs even before birth (or to be more exact, follicles which will mature into eggs). As time goes by, the number and the quality of these follicles (potential eggs) dwindles, and this can be tracked by the presence of FSH. Normal levels of FSH in the urine at that point of the cycle indicate normal fertility – the eggs are of a quality and number that indicate no real concern. A raised level of FSH indicates that the chances of the egg being fertilizable are reduced (but not necessarily impossible). The test in current use takes about 30 minutes to work.

For men, the standard sperm assessment has traditionally been done in a clinic. A semen sample is produced, and then analyzed by counting (or calculating) the number and quality of sperm per millilitre. The sperm need to motile (that is, moving), and to be of a normal structure. Unusual tails or other anomalies make it more difficult for the sperm to get up the vagina, into the uterus and beyond to fertilize the egg.

The home test is a quick assessment, which takes a few minutes to be effective. You place the sample in a device which puts the sperm through their paces – they have to swim through a chemical barrier which imitates the mucus and the environment of the female cervix, just as they would have to do after ejaculation. The number of sperm who reach the 'other side' can then be counted, and the 'sperm per mil' level is calculated. You can then read off the result, using the visual sign on the outside of the device, which gives a positive result if the number is normal. In fact, this test is better than the standard lab test because it's actually simulating 'real' conditions. It also uses the whole of the ejaculate and not just a portion of it, so results may even be more accurate than a lab-based test.

Other kits test in a different way, checking the concentration of sperm in a small amount of semen only. Samples are placed in a dropper, and drops of semen go onto a test card. They are then stained with a colour, and the intensity of the colour is compared with a standard – a positive result shows a normal sperm count of above 20 million per millilitre. You would normally be advised to wait 3–7 days, and to repeat the test then. In fact, all tests currently on the market suggest more than one test. This makes results more reliable, allows you to improve the way you follow the instructions, and helps to avoid the chance of a misleading result.

Some drugs and medications can affect your sperm count, and alcohol intake may also have an impact – men's sperm counts go up and down with their health, their activity levels and their intake of alcohol or other drugs. Bear in mind that, while most men will stay well within normal fertility levels whatever they do, it could make a difference if you're more borderline.

Remember!

A test like this doesn't check for other aspects of fertility, like problems with fallopian tubes.

Abortion and fertility

Q. I had an abortion in my teens, and I'm now trying to become pregnant again. Is the abortion the reason it's taking so long?

A. Proper care after abortion would ensure any infection arising before or after the abortion would be treated, so no, there should be no effect on your fertility. If you're concerned though, speak to a doctor, and it's highly likely you will be reassured.

You should share with any fertility adviser the fact you had an abortion, however. It will help any decision on treatment, because you have demonstrated that you were fertile at that time.

RELIABILITY

Checking and tracking your fertility at home is known to be reliable, as long as you follow the instructions and are consistent about what you're doing.

None of the tests or charts done at home should be seen as diagnostic. They won't tell you what's wrong, if anything, though they can point to aspects of normality. They're more accurately thought of as 'screening' tests that indicate when further, possibly diagnostic, tests might be useful to do.

Your doctor or fertility specialist won't mind if you present him or her with your folder of charts and results – it's not thought of as stepping on their toes at all, and of course, this is your own body – or bodies – you're taking a closer look at!

Pros and cons

THE DOWNSIDE

It's up to you how far you go with fertility awareness. Some couples admit to getting very – maybe unnecessarily – keen on it, so all spontaneity is taken out of sex, which is a known drawback of prolonged fertility investigations.

Running a sperm assessment doesn't usually need to be done more than a couple of times, and once done, it's out of the way if everything appears normal and healthy. But tracking and checking ovulation needs more long-term, every-day commitment, and it can become boring and disheartening. You build your hopes up to that time you know you're ovulating more or less, and then you have that 'two-week wait' (the '2WW', as it's termed on the web forums) to see if you've managed to become pregnant.

There's also a financial cost involved – all home-testing apparatus bears some cost, although prices are falling over time, as kits become smaller and easier to produce.

THE UPSIDE

There are advantages, however, to all aspects of fertility awareness. There is a lack of spontaneity and a risk of almost obsessive behaviour when trying to conceive, and many couples will manage to achieve a pregnancy without being aware of their fertility at all; however, if you suspect you may have problems, or if you feel time is not on your side, being aware can cut valuable corners – and help you organize your life and your plans.

A home fertility test means you can present a doctor with an outline of your potential problems before you have gone several months or more with no successful conception. It also informs any subsequent investigations on both of you. If there is an issue with sperm quality or quantity, this can mean fewer or no invasive tests on the woman. Moreover, producing a sample at home can save awkwardness and embarrassment – and it's got to be easier than taking an afternoon off work to go to the clinic.

Fertility specialists are on the whole in favour of encouraging awareness, and home testing when it's wanted. It's not for everyone, however. If you're finding it's all a bit much, take a month or so off. In the long term, this won't make any difference, and having a break can ease any pressure you're feeling.

Q&A

A chance of twins?

Q. I would love to have twins. Is there any way of increasing my chances?

A. Non-identical twins – which are far more common than identical ones – happen when more than one egg is released at (or soon after) ovulation, and when they're both fertilized.

The tendency to ovulate twice per cycle seems to be inherited (which is why twins 'run in families', down the maternal line), but there is no way of knowing if and when you release two eggs per cycle. Twins are more likely to be born to older women (over 35), so that would increase the chance a little – but beyond that, it's chance and genetics.

Twins are a lot of fun, but hard work too, and twin pregnancy and birth is more challenging and has more risks than a singleton pregnancy – it's not all lovely! Clinically speaking, multiple births – including twins – can be a potential problem.

Identical twins are random – there's no hereditary aspect at all, and of course no way of increasing the chance of their conception.

Trying too hard?

Q. I hear from so many people that we're probably 'trying too hard' to become pregnant. Is there any evidence that this can be the case?

A. This is such an irritating thing to hear, it's no surprise it drives people crazy! There's certainly some sense in couples making a conscious decision to enjoy themselves, and not focus solely on conceiving, simply to be happier and have a more fulfilled and rich life. But there's really no reason why stopping trying 'too hard' (a mystifying notion!) should somehow change the way the body functions. Having said that, there are many, many instances of couples who decide not to think about it so much, even choose not to have any more children or starting adoption proceedings, who then become pregnant. Most couples experiencing fertility problems will conceive anyway, given enough time. The decision to 'stop trying' just coincided with when the conception occurred by chance. Probably!

It's possible the origins of the idea of 'trying too hard' are linked to a prevailing notion that frequent ejaculation in the man reduces his fertility – that if you ejaculate too often, 'demand' outstrips 'supply'. There is always semen, of course, but it has fewer sperm in it. Tests and research show that the quantity of sperm does vary from man to man, and within the same man on different occasions (it's one reason why sperm assessment sometimes asks for two samples, if the first sample looks 'borderline'). However, recent studies indicate that frequency of ejaculation does not account for the variation, or accounts for only a small part of it. It's generally not wide enough to make the difference between fertility and infertility in most men.

As for what to say when people use the phrase 'maybe you're trying too hard', that's up to you. 'Maybe you could mind your own business?' is an idea, but it might be a little too blunt...

THINGS TO REMEMBER

1 'Natural' contraceptive methods use fertility awareness; it's perfectly feasible to use the same principles in the opposite way, to make it more likely that you will conceive.

2 Sperm survive and remain capable of fertilizing the egg for 2–3 days (and even up to 7 days), and can be present before the egg is released.

3 If you go a long time without having sexual intercourse, you may be missing some or even all your chances to conceive in any given cycle.

4 True scheduling will mean making sure you have sex on day 13 of your cycle and for good measure, on both days either side of that too.

5 Women with a long menstrual cycle (more than 28 days) ovulate later in their cycle than women with a short menstrual cycle (fewer than 28 days).

6 Ovulation can still happen as early as day eight, or as late as day 16 or 17.

7 You can track your basal body temperature with a special fertility thermometer – temperature rises shortly after ovulation.

8 You can also check cervical mucus and the position and texture of your cervix for changes.

9 Ovulation predictor kits can help you pinpoint ovulation more accurately.

10 Use of the contraceptive pill should not affect your fertility in the long term.

5

Supporting your own fertility

In this chapter you will learn:
- *how lifestyle and environment can impact on your fertility*
- *about ways to improve your health*
- *about the research trying to ascertain if there is a direct link between these factors and fertility.*

Exploring ways to improve your fertility means making an active decision to change aspects of your life, and to maintain these changes long term. It's more than just aiming to encourage conception by getting on side with your own body's calendar. It's looking at your weight, your diet, your drinking patterns, drug and medication use – whether you're male or female, any of these and all of them can make a difference.

However, the evidence that these factors make a measurable difference in individual cases is hard to find. Some aspects of lifestyle have fairly robust research to back them up, as we'll see later. Others have only weak associations with fertility, others again may be shown in animal studies only, or they may be based on a simulation in the lab, not real life. Also, an association can sometimes be made between an environmental or lifestyle factor and a change in fertility – but this is not the same as saying one causes the other.

It's always going to be hard to specify cause and effect, when people with 'unhealthy' lives who have a diet, alcohol and drug habits that make a fertility specialist's hair curl become parents all the time, with apparently no problem or delay. Moreover, it's always going to be difficult when people with a history of fertility problems succeed in becoming pregnant without anyone doing or changing anything – it's as if time – pure and simple – has eventually allowed it to happen. And just to complicate things even further, when people do make changes, they sometimes tend to do it with a 'scattergun' approach (see Gill's story on p. 79). It is uncertain if it was Gill's nutritional supplements, her personal trainer, or the fact she stopped using sweeteners that made a difference, or if any of them did. Maybe she would have become pregnant anyway, even if she had made no changes at all.

Remember also that studies may show the positive or negative impact of certain behaviours, foods or substances on fertility, but that's not the same as showing effects on conception and pregnancy.

It's also easier to check for changes in levels of male infertility, because sperm counts and sperm quality are relatively easy to check – you just compare sperm samples before and after an intervention. Sperm samples are also simple and quick to obtain – assessing the effect on female fertility is a much more complex procedure. Ovulation can be tracked to a certain extent, but egg quality and function can only be assessed by removing the eggs at ovulation (or when ovulation is induced).

It's understandable that individuals, and couples, think hard about what might be stopping them from having a much-yearned baby. Is it something they're doing, or not doing?

The anger and disappointment can mean they look for aspects of their bodies they can control, in the hope that ensuring changes will have an impact on the way their bodies function, even in an unspecified, general way like 'being more healthy'.

Take heart from the fact it makes sense to optimize the way your body functions, to avoid ingesting something that impairs it, or to lose/gain weight in order to be closer to a healthy ideal. After all, there's never going to be any physical harm in taking these steps.

Insight

If you are having problems, it is worth taking control of your lifestyle and aiming to be healthier. It will not have a negative effect, you can be sure.

Diet

Most general advice about preparing for pregnancy will encourage you to have a 'healthy diet'. There's plenty of information about what this consists of, and your doctor can point you in the direction of a healthy eating leaflet or factsheet if you need one.

A diet that has everything it needs takes food from one of these groups on most days:

▶ **Bread and cereals,** *including pasta and rice, and potatoes. These are good sources of carbohydrate, protein and B vitamins, low in fat and filling. Try to choose high fibre, wholegrain varieties which contain more vitamins and minerals.*
▶ **Fruit and vegetables,** *fresh, frozen and tinned varieties, salad vegetables, beans and lentils, dried fruit and fruit juice. Eat at least five portions a day for vitamin C, carotene and some of the B vitamins; eat them as soon as possible after cooking, as the vitamin content is easily lost.*
▶ **Meat, fish and alternatives** *(eggs, nuts, pulses such as beans, lentils, chickpeas). Eat moderate amounts and choose lower fat versions whenever possible. These foods are a major source of protein, vitamins and minerals. Aim for at least one portion of oily fish (sardines or salmon, for instance) a week.*
▶ **Milk and dairy foods.** *Eat moderate amounts and opt for lower fat versions. They are high in calcium and protein.*

Skimmed and semi-skimmed milk contain just as much
calcium and protein as whole milk.
▶ **Foods containing fat and sugar.** *Eat in small amounts only.*

Adapted from *Bandolier* (www.medicine.ox.ac.uk/bandolier/),
the journal of evidence-based healthcare.

Certain nutrients have come under the spotlight either as
something to avoid, or as 'superfoods' to eat more of. The following
is very far from being an exhaustive list. Keep an eye on the
newspapers to stay up to date; the internet is often useful to read up
on the original research behind the news items, so you can make your
own mind up. Clips from papers and news stories about these foods
and nutrients are included below, for you to follow up if you wish.

Remember, not all studies are good quality, and just because
something appears in a medical journal, scientific magazine or
the science column of a newspaper, does not mean it's necessarily
significant, either for the general population or for you. It's good
that research is carried out in this field, but many things that look
like a breakthrough at first turn out not to be quite as exciting as
was thought at first.

Here are just some of the nutrients that may have an impact on
fertility:

▶ **Soya.** *Eaten by women, it may have a negative effect on*
sperm, because a compound can affect the way sperm behave,
and encourages them to 'peak' too soon, reducing their ability
to fertilize the egg by 'burning out'. Eaten by men, soya
reduces the quality of sperm, because it contains the female
hormone oestrogen which affects the way the sperm are
manufactured in the body.
▶ **Coffee.** *In men it can increase the performance of sperm by*
increasing their motility. In women, it reduces the chance of
conception.
▶ **Zinc.** *This is found in oily fish, sardines, some nuts and seeds,*
poultry, beef, lamb and whole rice. While a healthy diet will
not be short of it, you can survive on a diet very low in zinc,

but there's good evidence that a deficiency can affect fertility. Some studies show that, in men, zinc supplements boost the number of normal sperm. Zinc is also an important mineral for the female reproductive system, and some practitioners will advise women to increase their intake, either through diet or supplements.

▶ **Folate.** *This is the B vitamin found in dark green leafy vegetables and whole grains – again, a deficiency shouldn't be an issue if you're eating well, but supplementation has been shown to boost male fertility. Women planning to conceive are advised to ensure they take supplements – see Chapter 6 – for the developmental health of the foetus, and these are in addition to a healthy diet.*

▶ **Antioxidants.** *Examples of these are vitamins and other nutrients including Vitamin C, Vitamin E and co-enzyme Q10. They boost male fertility, apparently by reducing the sperm's tendency to agglutinate (clump together – clumped together sperm don't swim well).*

▶ **Vitamin C (ascorbic acid).** *This benefits women who have a luteal phase defect (whose hormone levels in the second half of the menstrual cycle are too low to sustain pregnancy).*

▶ **High protein.** *Atkins-diet type regimes may have a negative impact on female fertility.*

In the press – Soya 'link' to male infertility

Researchers in Belfast found that the humble soya bean may play a role in the problem of male infertility. Soya contains the female hormone oestrogen and too much of it is being linked to poor quality sperm.

BBC News, 24 February 2004

It is also believed that women should avoid eating too much soya if they're trying for a baby, as a study in humans has shown a compound in soya called genistein sabotages the sperm as it swims towards the egg.

Professor Lynn Fraser, from King's College London, said even tiny doses in the female tract could burn sperm out. She told a European fertility conference that avoiding soya around women's most fertile days of the month might aid conception.

BBC News, 21 June 2005

Antioxidants and male fertility

Guys, here's another reason to eat your veggies: they might be good for your sperm. Some studies show that male fertility and what's called seminal quality have declined over the last few decades. So researchers from two fertility clinics in Spain looked at the reproductive power of fruits and vegetables. The scientists have spent the past four years analyzing diet and possible exposure to workplace contaminants in men with fertility problems.

One effort examined the effects that antioxidants might have on sperm. The researchers hypothesized that antioxidants could lower the oxidative stress that can harm sperm. More antioxidants could theoretically improve both sperm concentration and motility.

Podcast, *Scientific American*, 2 June 2009

Insight
Research reported in the news on how various behaviours, foods and drinks are linked with fertility is often exaggerated.

Nutritional supplements

There are a number of studies which assess the effects of extra minerals, vitamins and other nutrients – usually in pill form – on fertility. There does seem to be a role for them, though we lack a large body of research which would really prove that they make a difference.

There are plenty of commercially packaged nutritional supplements on sale in pharmacies and health stores, as well as on the internet. It's illegal for advertising to be untruthful, and health claims have to be substantiated, which is why you should not see any products labelled as a 'cure for infertility' – you should sceptical about any manufacturer who would deliberately break the law in this way. Instead, products will tell you what their constituents are, and perhaps what function of the body they're intended to support, and they may even tell you what the ingredients are 'traditionally used for'. Manufacturers have to demonstrate their products are safe to use as directed, so they should not do you any harm.

Do they do any good though? It's a fact that modern-day diets are often poor, and the way foods are grown, manufactured, transported, stored and prepared can affect their quality. Twenty-first century people may have irregular eating habits, eating disorders, a full timetable, a preference for fast foods etc., so it's easy to see that a handy pill could plug some gaps and act as a sort of nutritional insurance policy, supplying nutrients that would otherwise be in short supply. As such, good quality supplements may well have a role in overall health.

Supplements are more than just a tightly packaged 'multi-vit', however. They may include specific antioxidants, or higher doses of one or more nutrient. Some private fertility clinics may sell their own formulations, specially made up to target sub-fertility in men and/or women.

It's not possible to say if they will 'work' for you or your partner. Are they worth a try? It's up to you – check out what research you can, as it's easier than ever before to do so, and discuss your findings with your advisers. Bear in mind they may have a financial interest in getting you to buy them, but that doesn't automatically mean they're ripping you off either.

A healthy weight

Women who are very overweight or underweight are likely to be less fertile than women of normal weight. Weight can have a major endocrinological (hormonal) effect on the body, related to the presence or lack of body fat.

Overweight women may have a hormone imbalance, which can make it harder to conceive and maintain a pregnancy. It may lead to irregular ovulation, or no ovulation. Women with a body mass index of over 30 (in a woman of 5 feet 4 inches [162 cm], that's about 12.5 stone [80 kg]) may find it harder to get IVF treatment because the procedure is less likely to be successful. The UK National Institute of Clinical Excellence (NICE) has a BMI of over 29 as a cause for concern with regard to fertility. (BMI is a number calculated from a person's weight and height. BMI provides a reliable indicator of body fatness for most people and is used to screen for weight categories that may lead to health problems.)

Being underweight affects ovulation, and women with very little body fat may not menstruate or ovulate.

Men too have been shown to be less fertile if they are overweight. Men with a higher body mass index (BMI) have been shown to be significantly more likely to be infertile than men of normal weight, according to research conducted at the National Institute of Environmental Health Sciences (NIEHS), one of the National Institutes of Health. 'The data suggest that a 20-pound increase in men's weight may increase the chance of infertility by about 10 per cent,' says Markku Sallmen, lead author on the paper, who is now at the Finnish Institute of Occupational Health (*Fertility News*, 2006).

Q&A

Passive smoking and fertility?

Q. I don't smoke, and neither does my partner. Could the fact
that both his parents and mine do smoke affect our fertility?
We visit them quite a lot, and both houses are very smoky. I
don't feel able to ask them not to smoke when we're around.

A. There is some research on this, and you might be wise to
be concerned. ASH (Action on Smoking and Health) have
a factsheet (at www.ash.org.uk) which details the evidence
for the effect of smoking on women's and men's fertility and
reproductive health.

There's a lot of epidemiological evidence – the sort of research
that looks at patterns of illness or in this case fertility problems,
and the circumstances in which these problems occur. This
shows that both men and women have lowered fertility when
they're exposed to passive smoking, perhaps because they have
a smoking partner or because people at work smoke. If you're
with your parents a lot, this might be the equivalent.

Exactly how smoking might have an effect on fertility is less
clear, but there is enough research for you to think about
putting your collective feet down and asking them to refrain.
You will have even more reason to do so if you become
pregnant, and yet even more if they want their grandchild to
visit. A smoky atmosphere is not good for a foetus or a baby.
Perhaps you can practise your assertive techniques now!

Alcohol and nicotine

Smoking and drinking have a marked effect on male and female fertility, and as each can have an effect on pregnancy, and the health of the foetus and the baby after birth, this is a good time to think about quitting smoking, and at least cutting down on alcohol. Some fertility specialists advise no alcohol at all in the pre-conception period (guidance changes – ask your doctor and keep reading the newspapers).

OTHER DRUGS

'Street' drugs have not been widely studied for their effect on fertility, but some are known to be harmful in pregnancy.

There are some animal studies that indicate marijuana as a cause of ovulation problems.

An interesting experiment carried out by the Open University's 'Lab Rats' for the BBC (www.open2.net/labrats) compared two healthy males for sperm quantity and quality, over the course of a week. One man deliberately reduced his sperm count by eating poor food, drinking more alcohol and wearing tight underpants (to increase the temperature of his testicles, known to have an effect on sperm production). It worked – he 'lived like a slob', in his own words, and decreased his fertility, while his counterpart took simple measures to live better for just a week, and increased his.

Stress and anxiety

Interesting work has been done on helping infertile women learn to relax and improve their mental health, with some promising results. 'Sub-clinical' effects of stress – that is, the sort that don't show – can, it appears, interfere with the menstrual cycle and ovulation, and treating stress with relaxation or behavioural therapy may amend and improve this.

It's well documented that in men also stress can interfere with the production of sperm; men who suffer from stress and/or anxiety may find it hard to obtain and maintain an erection too.

Treatment of stress has been suggested as a first step in assisted reproduction (IVF and other treatments), with a view to having a successful outcome with fewer attempts.

Some studies show that programmes to deal with stress can restore normal menstruation and ovulation, and improve sperm counts. The research is strong enough to discuss stress reduction with your doctor or clinic and to get a medical opinion on whether it might help you.

Insight

If you think, or you have been told, that stress is a health issue for you, there may be different ways to reduce it. Simple changes to your everyday life can make a difference.

Sperm quality down?

Press reports in recent years announcing a dramatic lowering of sperm quality and quantity in today's men have been based on concerned scientists' comparison of data from today and 30-odd years ago. Commentators, scientific and otherwise, showed scepticism at this (the old data was not as robust as it should have been) and the truth is, we really can't be sure if male infertility is on the rise or not.

If it is, there are plenty of ideas being thrown around as an explanation. All the following lifestyle factors – and many more – have been shown in studies to affect sperm quality and/or quantity, whether or not they are responsible for the modern-day fall (if indeed it is a genuine one):

- *an increased use of laptop computers*
- *radiation from frequent flying*
- *disposable nappies worn as an infant*
- *pesticides and other contaminants in foods or in the workplace*
- *everyday pollutants affecting the way the body functions*
- *plastics used to wrap foodstuffs which leach into the foods*
- *hormones in drinking water*
- *stress and pressure in the workplace*
- *traffic pollution*
- *use of mobile phones*
- *phthalates in cosmetics and deodorants*
- *being born to a mother who ate a lot of beef*
- *iodine in salt*
- *hot baths and jacuzzis*
- *tight underwear*
- *long-distance driving or sitting in an office for lengthy periods.*

Some of them you can do something about, but you can't control how much beef your mother ate before you were born, what sort of nappies she put you in, or whether the salt you've added to your food for a couple of decades or more has had iodine in it.

Even so, a few changes are easy enough, and have some easily accepted logic to them as well. Testicles are outside the body because sperm manufacture works best just below body temperature. If you can adapt your life so this isn't undermined, you'll support the natural processes more effectively – loose underwear (like boxer shorts) is the first thing often suggested to men asking about fertility boosts.

What does this mean for you and your partner?

Trying to get pregnant can feel like a full-time job – the emotional and practical impact of it is discussed at more length in Chapter 15, but even if we look at 'simple' lifestyle adjustments in diet, fitness and exercise, it's clear these also can take a lot of effort, commitment and time. Debbie Taylor's protagonist Sylvia, in her novel *Hungry Ghosts*, tries to get pregnant and to stay pregnant by keeping a watch on everything she eats and drinks… and it's laborious.

> *Her period comes and goes. There are daffodils in Sainsbury's.*
>
> *It's taking her longer and longer to do the shopping. She's made a list of teratogenic food additives and has started reading the labels on everything she buys. She searches for certified GMC-free oats, and coffee decaffeinated with water instead of chemicals.*
>
> *One Saturday, she's away so long, Bennet goes looking for her. He finds her at the dairy counter with an empty trolley, picking up one pack of cheese after another, trying to remember which are possibly infected with listeria.*
>
> *'Do you know what time it is?' He takes a slice of brie from her hand and puts it back on the shelf. 'You've been in here three hours.'*
>
> *'I wanted some cheese for tonight.'*
>
> *'It doesn't matter. We can have something else.'*
>
> *'There weren't any organic carrots so I can't do that casserole. I asked the fish man about the salmon and he's gone to ask someone where it's from.'*

... people are nudging at her with heaped
trolleys. How can they eat all that stuff?
Emulsifiers and stabilizers. Hydrogenated fat.
Permitted colourings. Aspartame.
Her scalp feels hot, as though she is wearing a
tight beret. Has she really been here for
three hours?

Hungry Ghosts by Debbie Taylor (Penguin, 2006)

Lifestyle changes are never easy. Losing weight is one such change that many people find particularly challenging. If it was easy, no one would be making money from slimming clubs, slimming pills, or liposuction and other 'fat busting' operations. Keeping the weight off is even harder – the vast majority of people who lose weight put it all back again and more once they stop their weight-loss diet.

Smoking and drinking are habits that are hard to break too. Finding the right treatment, if it's needed, for stress and anxiety, may need some searching, plus some commitment to working less and playing more.

Changes to overall health and fitness – like deciding to work on your weight, fitness and alcohol, nicotine and drug use – are worthwhile doing in themselves, whether or not they result in pregnancy. But you will need to support each other, and possibly to find other support, as you carry them out. Don't let anyone kid you it's simply a case of will power or wanting a baby strongly enough. You may need to seek the help of a doctor or other specialist to help you make the changes you want.

Insight

It's exhausting trying to be perfect, and it can be annoying when people who are very far from perfect have no problems conceiving. Life, and the creation of life, can be distressingly unfair.

I made loads of lifestyle changes – the first one was when I got a personal trainer and lost three stones (20 kg), then I relaxed and put a whole stone (6 kg) back on. I used the Zita West books over 12 months and I took loads of her supplements; I stopped all my caffeine intake, and took in no alcohol, no aspartame or saccharin; I didn't dye my hair; and I even stopped using my electric blanket. Finally, I went for reflexology in the lead up to embryo transfer. You could say it was the shotgun approach really – maybe I was clutching at straws but the transfer was successful!

(Zita West is a private practitioner, and the author of many books and articles about natural ways to support fertility. She has a clinic in London.)

Interesting findings to consider

'Caffeine consumption does not independently affect the probability of conception, but may enhance alcohol's negative effect.'
Alcohol and caffeine consumption and decreased fertility.
Fertil Steril. 1998 Oct;70(4):6327

'Our findings suggest that especially non-smoking women who wish to achieve a pregnancy might benefit from a reduced caffeine intake.'
Caffeine intake and fecundability: a follow-up study among 430 Danish couples planning their first pregnancy.
Reprod. Toxicol. 1998 May–Jun;12(3):289–95

'Total normal sperm count increases after combined zinc sulfate and folic acid treatment in both sub-fertile and fertile men.'
Effects of folic acid and zinc sulfate on male factor sub-fertility: a double-blind, randomized, placebo-controlled trial.
Fertil Steril. 2002 Mar;77(3):491–8

(Contd)

'Numerous antioxidants such as vitamin C, vitamin E, glutathione, and coenzyme Q10, have proven beneficial effects in treating male infertility.'
Mechanisms of male infertility: role of antioxidants.
Curr Drug Metab. 2005 Oct;6(5):495–501

'...vitamin C supplementation can increase serum progesterone levels and increase the pregnancy rate in women with luteal phase defect.'
Effects of ascorbic acid supplementation on serum progesterone levels in patients with a luteal phase defect. *Fertil Steril.* 2003;80:459–61

'Women on the Atkins diet or sportswomen on a high-protein diet might want to consider changing their eating habits if they are trying to conceive. Animal studies suggest protein-rich diets lower fertility.' High-protein diet, low fertility.
New Scientist, 3 July 2004

'This study may offer some evidence for the hypothesis of adverse effects of pesticide exposure on time to pregnancy, but more research is needed to elucidate these effects.'
Time to pregnancy among female greenhouse workers.
Scand J Work Environ Health. 2006 Oct;32(5):359–67

'Nutritional supplements could provide an alternative or adjunct to conventional fertility therapies.'
Double-blind, placebo-controlled study of Fertilityblend: a nutritional supplement for improving fertility in women.
Clin Exp Obstet Gynecol. 2006;33(4):205–8

'This study showed that vitamin C supplementation in infertile men might improve sperm count, sperm motility and sperm morphology, and might have a place as an additional supplement to improve the semen quality towards conception.'

Improvement in human semen quality after oral supplementation of vitamin C. *J Med Food.* 2006 Fall;9(3):440–2

'Alcohol intake... was unassociated with infertility among younger women, but was a significant predictor for infertility among women above age 30...'
Alcohol use as predictor for infertility in a representative population of Danish women. *Acta Obstetricia et Gynecologica Scandinavica* 2003;82:744–9

'Our findings do not support the hypothesis that alcohol and caffeine impair ovulation to the point of decreasing fertility. The association between soft drinks and ovulatory disorder infertility seems not to be attributable to their caffeine or sugar content, and deserves further investigation.'
Caffeinated and Alcoholic Beverage Intake in Relation to Ovulatory Disorder Infertility. *Epidemiology* 2009;20:3

THINGS TO REMEMBER

1 *Exploring ways to improve your fertility means making an active decision to change aspects of your life, and to maintain these changes long term.*

2 *The really powerful evidence that lifestyle changes make a measurable difference in individual cases is hard to find.*

3 *Studies may show an impact, positive or negative, of certain behaviours or foods or substances on fertility, but that's not the same as showing effects on conception and pregnancy.*

4 *The internet is often helpful to allow you to read up on the original research behind news items, so you can make your own mind up.*

5 *Things that initially look like a breakthrough can turn out to be not quite as exciting as was at first thought.*

6 *Women who are very overweight or underweight are likely to be less fertile than women of normal weight.*

7 *Men with increased body mass index (BMI) have been shown to be significantly more likely to be infertile than normal-weight men.*

8 *Both men and women have lowered fertility when they're exposed to passive smoking.*

9 *Some fertility specialists advise no alcohol at all in the pre-conception period.*

10 *Treatment of stress has been suggested as a first step in assisted reproduction.*

6

Pre-conception care

In this chapter you will learn:
- *how alcohol should be regarded during pre-pregnancy and pregnancy*
- *the importance of folate when you're preparing for pregnancy*
- *about other essential aspects of pre-pregnancy health.*

There is evidence that the state of your health at the time of conception and all the way through pregnancy can have an impact not only on your health and your ability to manage the extra physical and emotional stressors of pregnancy, but also on the health and growth of your baby. The idea that for long-lasting good health you should 'choose your parents wisely' has an increasingly convincing basis in research – but not just with regard to inherited diseases or your propensity to them, or whether or not they can help you grow in good health because of material comforts and access to healthcare. In fact, there are many studies exploring the idea that the health of the mother in pregnancy and pre-pregnancy may have a long-lasting impact on the health of the baby not just in pregnancy or at birth, but also into childhood and adulthood.

Pre-conception care is increasingly seen as a public health priority in a number of countries. In the US, the Recommendations to improve preconception health and health care (issued by a government select panel in 2006) include guidance that 'each woman, man, and couple should be encouraged to have a reproductive life plan' and maternity care should include 'one pre-pregnancy visit for couples and persons planning pregnancy'.

The 'foetal origins of adult disease' theory used to be known as the 'Barker hypothesis'; it posits that a malnourished mother at the time of conception, and at various crucial moments after that when the foetus's need for good nutrition is at a high point, may end up with a baby who grows to be at risk of a number of conditions, principally heart disease and other degenerative illnesses.

Insight

There is a link between the ability to conceive and the ability to sustain a pregnancy – becoming pregnant is only half the story.

Nutrition

'Poor nutrition' is easy to spot if a mother is chronically underweight, goes through regular periods of deprivation or may be anaemic. This seriously low-level of nutrition is rare in the developed world, which has made it hard for researchers to work out precisely what might be needed to optimize pre-pregnancy and pregnancy nutrition, and to show how it might make a difference in individual women and babies.

On top of that, effects of health and lifestyle are only really visible at a population level – you can't make many – or any even – firm predictions for an individual. That's one of the reasons why some dogmatic messages to women about what you 'should' and 'should not do' in pre-pregnancy may be misplaced.

In the press – Nutritional intervention and folate supplementation

'There's growing consensus that appropriate food and nutrition-based interventions may substantially improve the health of mothers and their infants. However, the quality and extent of evidence applicable to women of childbearing age in developed countries is limited, and therefore the precise nature of the intervention required remains unclear.

Results from programmes of folate supplementation and from broader-based food supplementation programmes are promising, however.

There is strong evidence that nutrition before and during pregnancy is important for the health of the child, however the exact mechanisms by which this influence is exerted are not yet fully understood.

Interventions beginning after the first 6–10 weeks of pregnancy are less likely to produce the desired effect for that particular pregnancy. Nutrition interventions which occur earlier in pregnancy or during the pre-conception period are more likely to benefit mother and infant.'

From *Health Scotland*, Evidence into Action, 2005

Folate/folic acid

Folate is a B vitamin found naturally in many foods. Supplementary folate, called folic acid – over and above what you will find in food – is known to reduce the risk of the foetus developing neural tube defects (these are the conditions that result from failure of the spine to develop, such as spina bifida). As an adequate intake of folate has been discovered to be crucial to the development of the spine, women who increase their intake of folate at the time of conception and in early pregnancy have been shown to lower their risk of having a baby with a neural tube defect (NTD). More recent research indicates that it may have a role in protecting babies from developing heart defects too, and it appears to reduce the risk of pre-term birth.

You can find folate in a number of foods:

- *breads, including wholegrain breads and breakfast cereals (they may also be fortified with folic acid as well – you can check the label)*
- *green vegetables, such as cabbage, sprouts, kale, spinach*
- *beans and pulses*
- *oranges and orange juice*
- *yeast and beef extracts*
- *parsnips*
- *baked beans*
- *eggs*
- *potatoes*
- *yoghurt*
- *wholemeal pasta*
- *brown rice.*

However, research shows that for most women getting the amount of folate they need for the protective effect is quite difficult without a supplement. It's for this reason women are advised to take a daily 400 mcg (microgram) folic acid supplement every day in tablet form – these are not expensive, and they're widely available in chemists, supermarkets and health stores. Your doctor can also prescribe them, and if you don't pay for your prescriptions, then you won't have to pay anything for the supplements.

You may also be taking a multi-vitamin supplement, but it's unlikely to have as much as 400 mcg in it, so take the folic acid supplement as well. There's no risk in taking both, as the body gets rid of any excess it doesn't need.

Insight
Speak to your doctor about taking folic acid supplements
when you begin trying for a baby.

Drinking and smoking

Some changes to your pre-conception health and nutrition are
worth doing, and there's no argument about them. Stopping
smoking, choosing smoke-free environments, and reducing alcohol
intake are measures that are not controversial. Smoking and
passive smoking are known to have risks to the development of the
foetus; the risk of miscarriage increases; the rates of stillbirth and
neonatal death are also higher in smokers – but bear in mind it's
impossible to assess the link for any one individual.

There is some debate on whether pregnant or would-be pregnant
women should do more than reduce alcohol, and that instead
they should avoid alcohol completely – total abstinence is the US
Surgeon General's advice, but advice elsewhere is not as clear cut. In
2007, the official advice in the UK changed, to advise a zero alcohol
intake for mothers planning a pregnancy and for women actually
pregnant. The advice included an acknowledgement that there was
no real science to link low to moderate intakes with problems, and
nothing to suggest that no alcohol made any positive difference.

It seems to be the case that binge drinking (large amounts of
alcohol) can be potentially more harmful in early pregnancy.
There's also evidence that some mothers are more susceptible to
harm in the first weeks of pregnancy. Miscarriage rates are
higher in women who have binged on alcohol, and we know
that Foetal Alcohol Syndrome can be the result of heavy drinking
throughout pregnancy.

The safest approach, given that we don't know the 'safe' upper
limit, is therefore to have no alcohol at all, or to keep it to a
minimum (one or two drinks once or twice a week) especially in

the very early weeks. However, there seems to be no research-based reason why this should be more than a low-key guideline, and not a prohibition.

Alcohol consumption and the outcomes of pregnancy

'There is an increasing body of evidence suggesting harm to the foetus from alcohol consumption during pregnancy. While the safest approach may be to avoid any alcohol intake during pregnancy, it remains the case that there is no evidence of harm from low levels of alcohol consumption, defined as no more than one or two units of alcohol once or twice a week.

Binge drinking in early pregnancy may be particularly harmful and specific advice to young men and women should make this clear.

Advice on the risk of harm to an unplanned pregnancy, as well as the risk of sexually transmitted diseases, should be widely available. Access to postcoital contraception and screening for sexually transmitted infection should be made available to those whose behaviour has put them at risk.'

From Royal College of Obstetricians and Gynaecologists,

Statement, March 2006

Case study – Anne

I stopped drinking, I started taking folic acid, and I tried to make sure I was eating well, right from the start of trying to conceive. I was out the other night with some friends, and one of them was pregnant, and she'd carried on drinking – I couldn't believe it. I felt she should know better. Seems to me it's not worth taking a risk.

Q&A

Did my drinking put my baby at risk?

Q. We've been trying for a baby for three years, and now I think I might be pregnant at last. But I'm scared, because we went to a friend's wedding, and I got quite drunk – not incapable, but certainly drunker than I usually get. It was after we had decided not to focus on conception, and just let things take their course. So I was trying to live normally, and 'normal' for me is to over-indulge once in a while. Now I'm actually frightened to be pregnant in case I miscarry and then blame myself.

A. Concerns about having the perfect life and lifestyle for pregnancy are common among all prospective mothers – you might find that people without fertility concerns would feel the same way as you. Many women become pregnant after drinking a lot – some of them become pregnant as a result of it, because they don't bother with contraception... and their babies are just fine. Miscarriage and pregnancy loss happen all the time, and it's only when many thousands of women are studied that any possible link with binge drinking emerges. The odds of any one individual miscarrying because of this and no other reason are tiny. If you are pregnant, take an opportunity to speak to a midwife in confidence about your worries, and she will explain how very small the chances are that you have done any harm.

Insight

There is a potentially major difference between binge drinking and moderate social drinking, but this is not reflected in official advice.

Other drugs

RECREATIONAL DRUGS

The research on the use of recreational drugs pre-pregnancy and early pregnancy is not very vast, but a number of drugs are known to be teratogenic (harmful to the foetus). The safest option is, undoubtedly, to not use any.

PRESCRIBED DRUGS

If you need to take medication, or undergo medical or dental treatment, then let the doctor, dentist or pharmacist know you're aiming to conceive. Most medication is safe, and some drugs are known to be safe because research has been done with pregnant women. However, a few are known to be unsafe, and the decision would have to be taken to suspend medication if it was felt to be incompatible with pregnancy. On the other hand, some medication is safe as long as you are monitored.

For example, a long-standing condition such as epilepsy might be controlled by medication, and suspending medication might mean an increased risk of seizures, which may be risky in pregnancy. Speak to whichever specialist is caring for your condition and discuss your options, including the possibility of changing to a different medication.

USE OF THE CONTRACEPTIVE PILL

You can try for a baby as soon as you come off the pill, but it may be your cycle doesn't spring back to normal straight away. Some therapists maintain that there are nutritional effects of oral contraception. A healthy choice, they say, would be to come off the pill 3–6 months before trying to conceive, to overcome any deficiencies with a better diet and to increase the chances of a happy, healthy pregnancy. This is not mainstream advice, so ask your doctor or your clinic what their opinion is.

Mental health issues

Stress, depression and anxiety affect your own health during pregnancy as well as the baby's weight and health – several studies link mental health issues with difficult pregnancy, low birth weight in the baby, postnatal depression and symptoms such as excessive crying in the baby. Not all of this is certain to be cause and effect – if you're depressed during pregnancy, you may also be depressed afterwards, but that doesn't mean your antenatal depression caused you to have postnatal depression. It doesn't mean that if you get successful treatment for your depression before the baby's born, you're certain not to get postnatal depression afterwards. It could also be that a baby who cries a lot after birth is in some way responding to his or her mother's distress, rather than coming into the world 'pre-disposed' to crying because of being affected by stress while in the womb.

However, stress in pregnancy is known to have a physiological effect and may impair the way the placenta nourishes the baby – hence the tendency towards a low birth weight.

If you feel stressed, or in poor mental and emotional health, think about getting help and support with this, as part of a pre-pregnancy care programme – not just for your baby, but for your own sake too.

Pre-conception care for men

Healthy choices to boost your fertility are covered in Chapter 5. Alcohol, smoking and recreational drugs have been shown to affect the quality of sperm, as well as the quantity. Poor quality sperm are less likely to achieve fertilization, but there's very little solid evidence that men's health at the time of conception contributes to the health of the pregnancy. Clinics and specialists are likely to encourage men as well to adopt a healthy lifestyle, not just to support conception, but to 'cover all bases' when it comes to aiming for a positive outcome – a pregnancy that leads to the birth of a healthy baby.

Insight

Men who are in poor health may be less fertile, but this does not appear to mean any pregnancy is more at risk, should their partner conceive.

In the press – Women trying for a baby told to watch their diet

A study of more than 12,000 women aged 20 to 34 who were followed for four years found those who became pregnant were only marginally more likely to have followed recommendations on smoking, alcohol consumption and folic acid intake than their non-pregnant peers. More than three-quarters of the 238 women who became pregnant had planned their pregnancy to some degree, but there was little difference between their lifestyle and that of the women who had not planned to conceive.

Professor Hazel Inskip, an epidemiologist at the Medical Research Council Centre at the University of Southampton and lead author of the study published in the British Medical Journal, said: 'The foetus is particularly vulnerable in the first few weeks. Early influences affect the risk of miscarriage, may contribute to the obesity epidemic, have an impact on IQ and all sorts of subtle long-term effects.

'How we protect the next generation is very important. Parents want the best for their children, but people get more twitchy once their children are alive. Society needs to be thinking about this earlier.'

The Independent, 13 February 2009

THINGS TO REMEMBER

1 *The state of your health at the time of conception, and all the way through pregnancy, can have an impact on the health and growth of your baby.*

2 *Women who increase their intake of folate at the time of conception and in early pregnancy have been shown to lower their risk of having a baby with a neural tube defect (NTD).*

3 *Women are advised to take a daily 400 mcg (microgram) folic acid supplement every day in tablet form.*

4 *Miscarriage rates are higher in women who have binged on alcohol.*

5 *If you need to take medication, or undergo medical or dental treatment, let the doctor, dentist or pharmacist know you're aiming to conceive.*

6 *Stress, depression and anxiety affect your pregnancy health and have an effect on the baby's weight and health.*

7 *Clinics and specialists are likely to also encourage men to adopt a healthy lifestyle.*

8 *You can try for a baby as soon as you come off the pill, but it may be your cycle doesn't spring back to normal straight away.*

9 *A number of recreational drugs are known to be teratogenic (harmful to the foetus).*

7

Seeking help

In this chapter you will learn:
- *the length of time you might expect to wait before asking for medical help to conceive*
- *how your age and personal circumstances might affect how quickly investigations will be offered*
- *what initial fertility assessments might be looking for.*

Estimates vary, but most healthy, fertile couples where the woman is under 40 and having regular sex without contraception will conceive within a year – and a woman under 35 will take on average 4–6 months to conceive. The chances of conception per cycle for her are about one in four, if she ensures she has sex during the most fertile time (see Chapter 4).

Those statistics are averages, and not everyone is averagely healthy, averagely fertile, or having sex at the same frequency. Maybe about one couple in every six has a 'problem' with conception, or with carrying a baby to term. This may mean nothing more than a delay in conceiving, and that time itself will do the job, or it may mean one or both of a couple is infertile with no possibility at all of having a baby (very rare).

Fertility is more of a spectrum – some people are very fertile and conceive easily, and others have serious problems, with most people finding themselves at some point in between those two extremes. That point will change with age, state of health, and with different partners. That's why there is no simple answer to the question: 'When do we seek help to have a baby?'

A rough rule of thumb would be that unless you know there's a problem with your fertility already, you're probably best advised to wait a year before seeking medical advice if you're in your early 30s or below, and maybe six months if you are older than this (as there is less time to 'fix' problems before time starts running out). Some fertility specialists advise seeking help rather sooner than this, and would regard a few months at below the age of 30 as long enough to wait. This probably reflects the concern that some women are simply leaving things too long, and maybe relying too heavily on modern medicine to fix them. For women, it's true that time just isn't on your side, as we've seen in Chapter 1. Gill, in the case study later in this chapter, waited two years before seeking help after starting to try at age 34. Investigations showed she had untreatable blocked fallopian tubes. An earlier appointment would have revealed this sooner, and it's possible she may have reached specialist IVF help at an earlier time too.

Insight

See your doctor for advice if you have already become aware of potential fertility issues like irregular or absent periods, apparently irregular or absent ovulation.

Potential problems

Obvious problems you may already be aware of include:

▶ *you don't have regular periods*
▶ *your periods are infrequent*
▶ *you know you have a condition such as endometriosis or polycystic ovarian syndrome*
▶ *you have had a previous ectopic pregnancy*
▶ *you or your partner are unable to have normal sexual intercourse for some reason*

> ▶ *you or your partner are using prescribed medication which may have an effect on your fertility*
> ▶ *previous investigations have shown you have a problem.*

Your first port of call will be your general practitioner, who is the 'gatekeeper' for specialist help. He or she may have an interest in helping with fertility problems, and may have a special knowledge or extra training in it.

Some simple measures will probably come up as suggestions, such as scheduling sexual intercourse with fertility awareness techniques, and you'll be asked how long you've not used contraception and whether you've been pregnant before, or in the case of a man, made anyone pregnant before.

Your GP can refer you to a specialist clinic or doctor if you need further investigations or an opinion on whether you need them. There are many private clinics and some private specialists and clinics who treat clients well outside the mainstream – see Chapter 13 for an outline of what's available. But you don't need to 'go private'; treatment is available everywhere, though some techniques and interventions may not be offered to everyone. This may be on clinical grounds, because you or your partner (or both) are unlikely to benefit from it, or because there is a policy to put a 'cap' on the number of treatments permitted because of the cost. The cost issue collides with the clinical – how long, the argument goes, can public funds be on offer when they show no result? There are special interest or self-help groups who campaign for more resources and better training – even so, you may find your clinic can put you in touch with local or national group contacts for more information.

What happens when you seek help?

It's a good idea to turn up to your appointment as a couple (if you are in one), in fact you may be specifically asked to do so.

In the initial stages at least, you will be interviewed together, and it should be a sensitive and understanding process. 'Taking a history' is the start of any encounter, and it allows the doctor to be sure all the relevant information is there from the beginning.

You'll probably be asked very basic questions to rule out anything very simple – it's very rare that a couple present themselves without knowing how to 'make babies', but many doctors have a tale to tell about couples who were not aware and who needed some explanation.

The areas the doctor is likely to cover in this initial history taking include:

▶ *your general health and well-being, including possibly your weight, if you appear to be overweight or underweight*
▶ *your ages*
▶ *when you started your periods*
▶ *how frequent and how regular your periods are*
▶ *whether your periods are very heavy or light*
▶ *how many days you menstruate each cycle*
▶ *if you've ever been pregnant before and what happened*
▶ *if your partner has ever fathered a child and what happened*
▶ *what contraception you used and when you stopped*
▶ *what steps you have taken so far to increase the chances of conception (fertility awareness, change in lifestyle)*
▶ *if you've any pain or discomfort when you have sex*
▶ *if you're having sex at the more fertile time in your cycle*
▶ *any previous surgery and what the outcome of it was*
▶ *smoking and drinking habits*
▶ *whether any previous partners have gone on to become parents*
▶ *any history of sexually transmitted diseases.*

Many of these are likely to have been covered in your initial appointment with your family doctor, but you'll be asked them again, to confirm your answers.

You'll probably both have a physical examination, if not now, at some later stage. In this, the doctor will want to check:

▶ *that the testicles and penis appear normal*
▶ *that the prostate gland appears normal (assessed with a rectal examination). Sometimes, infections of the prostate can be a factor in fertility*
▶ *for any abnormalities of the uterus and pelvic organs, and to feel if there are obvious fibroids or adhesions (scar tissue that may remain after surgery or infection), or cysts (women may need more checks to see if any of these are present).*

Sometimes this history taking and the physical examination indicate the next step, and a good doctor will involve you both in any discussions about options, explaining exactly what any further tests are looking for, what any suggested or prescribed treatment is likely to do, and what the step after this next one may be.

If it helps you, ask the doctor to write down any advice and an outline of options if you need to discuss them later as a couple.

Insight

Some questions the doctor asks may seem very obvious or else irrelevant, but all the information is necessary for a full picture. If you see a fertility specialist, the same questions might be repeated – this is to check the information has been correctly recorded.

What next?

The answers that emerge from a discussion of your history and any findings of the physical examination will help point the way to the next step.

Further investigative checks may be necessary.

SPERM COUNT

A sample of sperm (obtained through masturbation, as this gives the fullest, cleanest sample) is collected in a container the clinic will issue you with. It's then kept warm and brought to the clinic or the clinic's lab, where technicians will look for any signs of infection, the amount of semen, the quantity of sperm per millilitre of fluid, their quality of movement, their structure and the amount of abnormal sperm. Sperm should be free to move and not clumped together (this is called 'agglutination').

The figures and observations will be compared to the normal range and, if there is a deviation, you'll probably be asked for a second sample, and possibly a third. This just reflects the fact that sperm quality and number are very variable, even in the same man. Weeks after an illness, for example, the sperm can show the effects. So you would be asked for a further sample after a couple of months have gone by.

POST-COITAL TEST

This may be carried out to see if the sperm are managing to get over the first part of the journey to the egg. Sperm that move poorly, that are fewer than normal in number, or which are not fully developed, will show up on this test, and the effect of the woman's cervical mucus is also shown. 'Hostile' mucus damages and kills the sperm so they can't get any further.

You'll be asked to have sex at about the time of ovulation, when cervical mucus is thin and stretchy (see Chapter 4) – not very spontaneous, it's true. The same day, or very early the next day, you'll go to the clinic, and will be asked to have a vaginal examination. The doctor or the nurse will remove a sample of mucus from the cervical canal (this should be painless or at least no more than slightly uncomfortable). The sample of mucus is put onto a slide so it can be examined by microscope and note whether it looks normal – thin, and like egg white.

The test may show that everything is normal, or that there's a possible problem with the sperm, and/or a problem with the mucus. Some women produce antibodies to the sperm which are present in the mucus; some men have similar antibodies in their own seminal fluid.

The problem is that although the post-coital test sounds as if it could be very useful, recent clinical practice and research indicates that it has very limited value. The same couple can produce very different results on different occasions, and it's simply not very good at predicting who can and who can't get pregnant together. Current NICE (National Institute of Health and Clinical Excellence) guidelines advise against its routine use, and many clinics no longer offer the test except in individual cases.

SPERM INVASION TEST

This test follows on from the sperm count, and may be done after the post-coital test. It gives a close-up view of what can happen to the sperm when it meets a mucus sample from the woman's cervical canal, but instead of it being done after sexual intercourse, the two elements of the test – sperm and cervical mucus – are brought together on a glass slide.

A drop or two of semen from a fresh sample is used (with the remainder of the sample being put into the cervical canal directly). The doctor or the technician can then look at what the semen is doing over a period of a quarter of an hour or so. The sperm should be able to penetrate the mucus in that time and then continue to move. If this doesn't happen, then it probably means there's some sort of chemical interaction that's preventing it. Antibodies in the sperm or in the mucus may be damaging the process of penetration. The clinic can look for these antibodies in blood samples taken from each of you.

Some doctors will do a further test with some known normal sperm, and some known normal mucus. This is called a 'crossover' test. This isolates the problem to one of the partners only.

HORMONE TESTS

These are sometimes known as hormone assays. We've already seen in Chapter 2 how fertility and specifically conception and the menstrual cycle are driven by hormones. The biochemical changes that take place in the male and female bodies are crucial to your chances of pregnancy.

The balance and relationship of hormones is complex. Everything needs to work in the right way, at the right time, and in the right quantity for conception to happen. By taking a sample of your blood at specific times in the cycle, specialists can tell a lot.

Hormone tests can look for follicle stimulating hormone (FSH), luteinizing hormone (LH), oestrogen and progesterone. If other hormones – notably prolactin – are present when they shouldn't be, these can affect the production of other hormones. You can also be checked for the appropriate level of thyroid hormone, as too much or too little can also affect fertility. Your production of progesterone should be at its highest three-quarters of the way through your cycle (if it's 28 days long) – this is about a week after ovulation. If there's a low level of progesterone, that's a strong indication that ovulation didn't happen in that cycle. The reason for this may be that the pituitary gland is not producing enough FSH or LH.

Men may have hormone levels checked as well, though the knowledge base and research into hormonal causes of infertility or sub-fertility is not great. It appears it's only very rarely that hormonal reasons cause male fertility problems, but research may reveal more in time.

Insight

It's fine to ask for the reasons behind any tests you are having done, and to ask when the results will be shared with you.

ENDOMETRIAL BIOPSY

NICE guidelines find no benefit to biopsy of the lining of the uterus. The lining is called the endometrium, and a small sample of it can be removed by the doctor by inserting a small instrument into the cervix which reaches the uterus lining. Cells can then be examined and compared to what they would normally look like at this stage of the cycle.

It is important to remember that you would need to be sure you were not already pregnant before you undergo this test, as the interference might affect the pregnancy. If you're offered it, ask what benefit is expected from it, and point out the lack of support from NICE for the procedure.

NICE guidelines also recommend screening women for chlamydia (a sexually transmitted disease) before any check on your fallopian tubes. If it's found you're infected, you and your partner (or partners) need treatment and subsequent follow up. Testing for chlamydia is quick and easy – it just needs a urine sample which is then sent to the lab for analysis.

FALLOPIAN TUBE, UTERUS AND CERVICAL INVESTIGATION

These are tests to check your fallopian tubes are 'patent' – that is, open – in order for the egg to make its way from ovary to uterus. There should be no abnormalities in the pelvic organs that would affect the journey. Blocked tubes can be a result of previous infection, fibroids, endometriosis (when endometrial material develops elsewhere than the uterus), or a previous ectopic pregnancy. Fibroids are benign tumours, non-cancerous growths made up of smooth muscle tissue, and they are very common. They grow in the uterus or on the outside, and while mostly women live with them without really being aware of them, they can cause pain, serious menstrual problems, bleeding and can interfere with conception.

Your doctor might advise one or more of a number of tests:

▶ **Transvaginal ultrasound.** *An ultrasound probe is placed in your vagina, and from there it can pick up a picture of your pelvic organs, which is then transmitted to a screen. The procedure is quite comfortable. The same procedure may be used during treatment, for example when eggs are retrieved for IVF or ICSI (see Chapter 13).*

▶ **Hysterosalpingogram.** *This test involves injecting a dye into the uterus and then seeing, on X-ray, where it goes. The dye should be able to fill the uterus and then go through both fallopian tubes and into the abdominal cavity. The way the dye behaves and where it goes can help diagnose where any blockages might be. You must not be pregnant when this test is carried out. However, as it's usually done in the first half of the menstrual cycle, the risk of pregnancy is not there. The procedure might cause some cramping at the time and afterwards. When it's over, the fluid is absorbed by your body and some of it comes out the vagina.*

▶ *Sometimes the procedure itself can help unblock the tubes, and recent work shows this is more likely to happen if an oil-based fluid is used. Your doctor can discuss this with you.*

▶ **Hysterosalpingo-contrast sonography.** *This is called 'HyCoSy' for short. HyCoSy uses ultrasound instead of X-rays to show the flow of the fluid through the uterus and tubes. One possible drawback with this test is that results may need to be clarified by laparoscopy instead, but it can be done without X-ray equipment, which makes it rather quicker and easier to arrange.*

▶ **Laparoscopy.** *This test lets the doctor take a direct look at what's going on in your pelvis. It's a surgical operation, performed under anaesthetic, and allows the insertion of a tiny scope on the end of a probe, which goes into a small incision under your navel. Your abdominal cavity is then filled with carbon dioxide gas to give a good view of the uterus, tubes and ovaries. The picture viewed by the scope is relayed to a screen and the doctor can observe if there are adhesions (scar tissue) affecting any of your organs, and other problems such as endometriosis and fibroids.*

The patency (openness) of the tubes is also tested during the procedure, by placing dye in the uterus and checking its flow.

The incision is easily closed up afterwards and you're left with virtually no scar.

▶ **Hysteroscopy.** *This check is similar to laparoscopy except the scope enters the uterus via the cervix. The uterus is inflated, and the doctor can see any unusual features or abnormalities, as with laparoscopy. It's a common investigation if fibroids are suspected, and minor fibroids can be removed at the time. Adhesions can sometimes be removed too.*

Treatment for fertility problems, based on what is discovered on investigation, is explored in Chapter 13.

Case study – Gill

After ten years together, we decided that the time was right to start thinking of having a family – I was 34 at the time.

After a couple of years of just letting nature take its course and not getting anywhere, we decided to take medical advice and the GP sent me for investigations.

They ended up finding I had blocked tubes. The prognosis was poor, and we were told treatment to unblock them would almost certainly be unsuccessful. I don't think the doctor was very sympathetic. He said our only chance was IVF – and that because I was by now almost 38, we were too old to be referred on the NHS.

We were given details of a private clinic who advised that I needed to lose at least five stones (32 kg) in weight and that I should only come back when I'd managed to do that. I tried and failed to lose a significant amount of weight over the next couple of years – I got depressed about it and it was easy to lose heart and think we'd never have a baby.

We decided to have another try at getting a different opinion. The GP was different and more sympathetic. He referred us to the Centre for Life* who said that we could go for IVF there and then.

Amazingly, I got pregnant first go but sadly, I had a missed abortion at 11 weeks.**

We had several more goes after that with no luck – I didn't even become pregnant.

We then moved house and changed our lifestyle – the plan was to accept that we would have a life together without children. There was one last frozen embryo*** and we decided to have one final attempt. Hey presto, I got pregnant aged 45, and we now have a beautiful little daughter.

* Newcastle Fertility Centre at Life, NHS funded unit based at the International Centre for Life in Newcastle upon Tyne. Leading clinic and research centre.

** See p. 159 for information about missed abortions.

*** If the mother is beyond her mid-30s, retrieving eggs before she becomes even older and then fertilizing them and storing them gives a higher success rate than relying on 'fresh' eggs.

Insight

It's helpful to do some of your own assessment on your scheduling of sex, and you can share with the doctor that you have this basic understanding of your fertility.

Treatment pathway

Investigations and assessments don't always happen in the same sequence, but this pathway is roughly what you and your partner may expect. Some general practitioners may refer you to a specialist clinic for the tests, and any treatment or invasive checks would normally be carried out after referral to a consultant.

1 *After a period of trying to conceive without success, see your GP.*
2 *Your GP will ask about your overall general health, how often you're having sex and when, and when you stopped using contraception. He or she may suggest scheduling intercourse and simple measures to monitor fertile times, plus advice on smoking, drinking, weight and other lifestyle issues.*
3 *The GP arranges for tests on sperm and hormone checks to assess ovulation, plus checks for infection.*
4 *Depending on these results, you may then be offered investigations to check your reproductive functioning, such as a check on your fallopian tubes and your pelvic organs.*

See Chapter 13 for what might happen next.

Q&A

How do I know what treatment I should have?

Q. We're about to seek advice on why we can't get pregnant. It feels like taking a big step, and I don't want to feel as if I'm not doing everything possible – on the other hand, how do I know what could be a waste of time?

A. A good specialist should be frank with you and explain what options you have and in what order they will be offered. It's also very useful for you to check things out yourself. The UK National Institute of Health and Clinical Excellence (NICE) is the organization responsible for establishing and assessing the clinical effectiveness of medical treatments and interventions, and they have a series of documents on fertility. The guideline 'Assessment and treatment for people with fertility problems' is available in full on the internet (www.nice.org.uk) for anyone to look at, but for most non-medical readers the version of it written for the public is clear and comprehensive. You can always also look at the medical details in the other documents as well, if you want to know more.

It's especially useful for explaining why certain investigations might be offered at a particular time, why some people might not have a certain test and why others might, and why you might be tested for something apparently unrelated to fertility at the same time (for instance, why women would have a smear test before any further tests, to make sure no treatment is needed for abnormalities of the cervix).

The guidelines are evidence-based, and you can have a good deal of confidence in them. Having said that, individual situations might justify a departure from the guidelines – they're not meant to be a blueprint for everyone.

THINGS TO REMEMBER

1 A woman under 35 will take on average 4–6 months to conceive.

2 About one couple in every six has a 'problem' with conception.

3 Unless you know there's a problem with your fertility already, you're probably best advised to wait a year before seeking medical advice if you're in your early 30s or below.

4 Seek help after six months if you are older than 35, as there is less time to 'fix' problems before time starts running out.

5 Your general practitioner is the 'gatekeeper' for specialist help.

6 Treatment is available everywhere, though some techniques and interventions may not be offered to everyone.

7 'Taking a history' is the start of any appointment, and it allows the doctor to be sure all the relevant information is there from the beginning.

8 Both men and women may be offered hormone tests.

9 Ask the doctor to write down any advice, and an outline of options if you need to discuss them later as a couple.

10 You can check current clinical guidance from the National Institute for Heath and Clinical Excellence (NICE).

8

Complementary and alternative help

In this chapter you will learn:
- *how best to seek help outside mainstream medicine or conventional fertility clinics*
- *about a variety of therapies available and what they claim*
- *how to find a practitioner.*

Mainstream treatments normally go through tests for safety and effectiveness. Studies will have been published in journals, and they will have invited comments and observations from colleagues. The work will be replicated by other practitioners and, at least in the UK, the results of interventions like IVF and ICSI are in the public domain, in terms of how many successful births result from the treatment. You can check up the performance of your clinic and compare it with others.

This may not be the case with other forms of help, the type you may get from alternative and complementary practitioners, sometimes described as offering 'CAM' (complementary and alternative medicine). This doesn't mean none of it works. But it does mean you need to be as cautious with this and to ask as many questions as you would with any other intervention.

Some CAM clinics are very costly, but again, this doesn't mean it's all a waste of money. But it doesn't mean it's certain to work either, and any good practitioner with a reputation to guard will make this clear. All of them will appear to have some successes, because sometimes, sub-fertility resolves itself spontaneously, without anyone doing anything at all. Women get pregnant after years and years of disappointment and heartache, after many different investigations, and often after giving up all hope. It just happens. The only way to be 100 per cent sure an intervention has actually caused the pregnancy is when fertilization has occurred outside the body, with IVF or ICSI, or if a clear obstacle (like blocked tubes, or an inability to have sex) is removed. Anything else could be coincidence.

Researchers in Bristol (see pp. 111 and 115) reported on the use of CAM by their patients, and pointed out some of the difficulties of doing good comparative studies. As they put it, there is 'a background chance of conception for most of the patients entering a clinical trial'.

Placebo-controlled trials are not possible, as you can't pretend to do acupuncture or reflexology in the way that you can give a sugar pill instead of a pharmaceutically active one. Case-controlled studies (where similar subjects are matched, except in one way, which would be the intervention of CAM) are a possibility, they say. But even getting treatment may have a 'placebo' effect as it could, they suggest, increase the number of times a couple have sex.

This isn't the book to assess the effectiveness of the many different therapies and interventions available – there are other sources of information that describe the details of what happens, and also suggest why certain therapies might work for you. While you should remain optimistic and upbeat, there are good reasons to be sceptical and to keep an eye on the price of it all.

Insight

Some fertility problems resolve by themselves: this may be the case for apparently successful results of either mainstream and complementary/alternative treatments.

Holistic approach

One feature of complementary therapies is that many of them take the time to look at your whole lifestyle and your entire body and mind rather than just the reproductive 'bits' of you – though this 'holistic' approach should not be outside the boundaries of conventional help either.

This may be supportive and encouraging, and help put you in control. It will ensure you think about stress and relaxation, your diet and your outlook. The Bristol researchers asked their patients why they accessed CAM. They found that a consultation with a complementary therapist was, on the whole, a positive experience in itself. Patients were happy to find someone who showed interest and who really listened.

Stress relief

Treating stress in order to increase the chances of successful pregnancy does have some evidence behind it – stress levels have been found to be higher in infertile women or in women who have been less successful with IVF. There may be some 'reverse causality' at work here, however – that is, they have elevated stress levels because of being infertile, and because IVF has not succeeded. Stress, nevertheless, does interfere with the body's optimum functioning – could this include your fertility? None of this is well studied, but because stress reduction and coping strategies will not harm you, either mentally or organically, then the worst that can happen is you risk building your hopes up.

Balancing the body

The NICE guidelines on assessment and treatment for people with fertility problems look at what works and what doesn't work and they say quite clearly: 'there have not been enough studies looking at complementary therapy treatments for fertility. Further research is therefore needed before any of these treatments can be recommended.' For more on the NICE guidelines, see p. 106.

The list that follows is an outline of just some of the therapies that cover fertility issues, with a brief indication of what is likely to happen with a consultation.

ACUPUNCTURE

This uses the careful (and pain-free) placing of needles in specific parts of the body to relax and/or stimulate it. There are a handful of studies showing some benefits to people undergoing fertility treatment. The basis of acupuncture is rooted in Far Eastern medicine, which believes that acupuncture stimulates and regulates the body's 'Qi' or energy. It's very different to the way Western medicine understands the way the human body works.

AROMATHERAPY

This uses essential botanical oils in massage, as a compress, or an inhalant. Aromatherapists claim to work on an emotional as well as a physical level to support and restore the body's own physiological functioning.

BACH FLOWER REMEDIES

These are homeopathically prepared medicines (i.e., diluted many times) which come from plant sources. They're used mainly to restore emotional and mental health, and to resolve negative attitudes.

BOWEN TECHNIQUE

A manipulating treatment, which involves hands-on contact with the muscles, tendons and ligaments to boost the body's own healing.

CHINESE MEDICINE

Traditional Chinese medicine (TCM) prescribes herbs which you take after mixing with water (and which are apparently sometimes unpleasant to taste) combined with acupuncture.

CRANIO-SACRAL THERAPY

A hands-on, very gentle manipulation which claims to make use of the way the cerebro-spinal fluid circulates round the brain and central nervous system. Like other therapies, it aims to restore balance in the body and stimulate the body's self-healing.

HAIR ANALYSIS

Some practitioners claim to be able to spot gaps in your nutritional health or an excess of minerals or toxins by doing analysis of a sample of your hair. They then aim to adjust this with advice on diet or supplements.

HERBALISM

Qualified herbalists claim that herbs can treat both male and female infertility and strengthen organs, including the pelvic organs. Herbs can be powerful and they can certainly have a biochemical effect on the body. Herbalists say they work with the body rather than against it, treating you holistically. They use the natural (not the synthetic) forms of the herb or plant.

HOMEOPATHY

This therapy claims that minute and untraceable quantities of a substance can stimulate the body to restore itself. Homeopathy believes that the more diluted the substance is, the more powerful its effect is – this claim certainly defies scientific investigation. Homeopaths have different remedies for different types of infertility and sub-fertility.

HYPNOTHERAPY

This aids relaxation and helps with a range of emotional and stress-related disorders. People undergoing fertility treatment may find it beneficial during an anxious time. You normally remain conscious and aware throughout the hypnosis session.

NATUROPATHY

This is a therapy that looks at diet and lifestyle, with the aim of restoring health through harmonious balance of everything you take in and everything you do. So there would be emphasis on wholesome nutrition, and avoidance of environmental hazards to try to create a healthy body for conception and pregnancy. Any medicines prescribed would be herbal or homeopathic; you might be advised to take nutritional supplements.

OSTEOPATHY, CHIROPRACTIC

Quite similar in the way they work, both these forms of therapy use pressure to amend the spinal vertebrae, and practitioners believe this doesn't just treat backache or other joint or muscle pain, but also other malfunctioning organs of the body.

REFLEXOLOGY

This therapy is used to bring about deep relaxation, by applying pressure to certain points of the hands and the feet. These points are claimed to have an affinity with other organs of the body.

SPIRITUAL HEALING

Used by people of all religions and none, treatment varies according to practitioner, and the spiritual or psychic aspect is very individual. Some practitioners do it by touch, others by holding the hands over or near the client; some claim to offer healing remotely, by prayer or meditation.

How popular is it?

CAM is widely used by people from all walks of life for just about
every ailment and condition there is, and that includes fertility issues.

Bristol medics working at a private Centre for Reproductive
Medicine and at St Michael's Hospital (NHS) surveyed 400 of their
patients who'd come to them for fertility investigations. They found
that 13 per cent of men and 40 per cent of women private patients
had sought out CAM; in the NHS clinic, the proportions were
11 per cent for men and 24 per cent for women (published on the
University of Bristol's ReproMed website www.repromed.co.uk).

In order of popularity, their patients had used:

1 *Reflexology*
2 *Acupuncture*
3 *Nutritional advice*
4 *Herbalism*
5 *Traditional Chinese medicine*
6 *Spiritual healing*
7 *Hypnosis*

A number of people used more than one (see Gill's case study in
Chapter 5).

Insight

You may be able to speak to other patients who have seen your practitioner and share experiences – ask if this is possible, though be aware that patient confidentiality will apply.

Finding a practitioner

Many complementary therapies have a professional organization – some have more than one. Membership is likely to mean the therapist has insurance, and some sort of qualification. If things go wrong (in the sense of you feeling unhappy about any of the procedures, rather than a disappointing outcome), you have a means of making a complaint, just as you can with mainstream medicine or nursing.

You can ask the practitioner about his or her credentials – no one worth your time and money would object to that, so don't be embarrassed – and many professional organizations publicize themselves on the internet, so you can send an email or make a call and do your own checks that way.

In the press – For seven years we tried everything to have a baby

Exclusive: I saw a Chinese herbalist as a last resort and gave birth to triplets!

Karen Styles and her fiancé Tony Maynard had endured two failed rounds of fertility treatment and were steeling themselves for a third when Karen fell pregnant naturally.

... And for Karen and Tony the greatest wonder of all is not the miracle of modern medicine, but a 2,000-year-old Chinese herbal remedy that seemed to do the trick. Karen and Tony, from Copthorne in West Sussex, were both tested for fertility problems but none were found. So, although she was sceptical, Karen visited Dr & Herbs in Crawley, and was given one session of acupuncture and a bottle of Chinese herbs for £35.

On 21 March 2007, eight weeks early, Thomas, Charlie and Antony were born by caesarean, all weighing less than 4 lbs. Karen says: 'They were in special care for four weeks until they put on more weight, but they were all healthy and gorgeous.'

Extracted from *Daily Mirror*, 2 May 2007

In the press – Herbal medicines 'may hinder IVF treatment'

Infertile women who supplement their fertility treatment with alternative medicines may be harming their chances of becoming pregnant, according to controversial research by psychologists. A year-long study of 818 women found that those who turned to complementary therapies such as herbal medicines, reflexology and acupuncture while having IVF treatment were at least 30 per cent less likely to become pregnant than women who did not.

A team led by Jacky Boivin, a psychologist at Cardiff University, investigated the effects of alternative therapies because they are increasingly being used by women undergoing fertility treatment. Some herbal treatments are marketed as natural remedies for infertility, while others claim to improve women's chances of getting pregnant by reducing their stress levels. Dr Boivin said it was unclear what was to blame for the apparent drop in pregnancy rates, but said the effect may be due to herbal medicines interacting with and disrupting drugs and hormones used in fertility treatment.

Guardian, 5 July 2007

THINGS TO REMEMBER

1 *You can check up the performance of your clinic and compare it with others, in terms of successful births.*

2 *Complementary and alternative medicine is less likely to have an evidence base than mainstream treatments.*

3 *Sometimes, sub-fertility resolves spontaneously.*

4 *Any form of treatment, complementary or mainstream, may have a placebo effect.*

9

....

Testing, testing...

In this chapter you will learn:
- *how pregnancy tests work and where you can obtain them*
- *when you can use a test*
- *other ways to confirm a pregnancy.*

Developments in testing

Just a little more than a generation ago, the usual way to find out for certain if you were pregnant was to watch the calendar for a few weeks, and then visit the doctor after you had missed two consecutive periods. Things have changed a lot since then.

In the 'old' days, the doctor would confirm your pregnancy, probably after you presented a urine sample, which would be sent away to the lab for testing. Within a week or so, you could phone the lab yourself, or your doctor's surgery, and get the result. By that time, you could easily be ten weeks pregnant.

Things became a little more streamlined about 30 years ago, when chemists offered pregnancy testing on the premises. Much was made of the fact that women could drop a sample of urine off at the start of their shopping and return an hour or so later and pick up the result. The test cost a few pounds – expensive compared to today's methods.

Then came the home pregnancy test, which has been widely and reasonably cheaply available for more than 20 years, and which you can pick up with your shopping in the supermarket. There's no real need for anyone to go to their doctor or chemist for a test, though you can if you want to; your doctor should agree to test if that's what you wish.

Other services offering tests tend to be aimed at reaching younger women needing pregnancy/abortion advice, and the offer of a quick, free test is partly a way to get them through the door, accessing the support available.

A common way to prepare for pregnancy these days is to buy pregnancy testing strips or sticks in large numbers, often over the internet, and to pay no more than a few pence for each one – prices are very low compared to the tests of the twentieth century, and no one these days would expect to have to wait until ten weeks of pregnancy before having it made 'official'.

Insight

Pregnancy tests are easy to carry out at home, cheap, and readily available anywhere – we have come a long way in a generation.

How do pregnancy tests work?

Whether you're using a home test or accessing a service, pregnancy tests work in the same way every time, by measuring the presence of a hormone called hCG – human chorionic gonadotrophin (sometimes termed chorionic gonadotropin without the 'h') in the urine.

When the embryo starts to implant in the lining of the uterus (see Chapter 3), something like a week or so after fertilization, the chorion (the structure that will become, in time, the placenta) starts to produce hCG. The main function of hCG in early pregnancy is to maintain the corpus luteum, stimulating its production of the hormone progesterone, which in turn supports the pregnancy.

The hCG hormone increases very rapidly in the first weeks of pregnancy. By the first day of your missed period, levels are high enough to be measured by a standard home pregnancy test, and they'll continue to rise until the end of the first three months. At that point they start to fall, though they will remain raised compared to when you're not pregnant, all the way through until your baby is born.

If urine containing hCG is placed on a pregnancy strip or stick, it reacts with an antibody in the strip or stick, which activates a dye. This results in the appearance of a coloured line, a dot, or a change in the colour of the end – different tests show results in slightly different ways.

Case study – Marion

The first time I became pregnant, I peed on the stick, and waited in the bathroom for the result, with my watch in my hand. My husband was waiting in the next room. It was exciting, as we were actively trying to conceive. It seemed unbelievable that it could happen on the first month! It was a bit of a scary moment – oh my god, it's happening, is it really what we want? Sadly, I miscarried later. When it came to getting pregnant again, I used the same brand of test, but this time I waited with my husband, not on my own. I told him to check the test as I couldn't face doing it myself.

When to test

Standard tests for use in the home are sensitive enough to react to hCG two weeks or so after conception, on the day you miss your period. This time is known on internet fertility support forums as the '2WW' or the two-week wait – the time between when you had sex trying to conceive, and the time you can test and expect a result, positive or negative.

Case study – Anne

It was the scientist in me – I tested straight away to find out, and actually expected a positive result because I'd planned the timing of it so carefully. I know it doesn't work that way for everyone!

However, there are even more sensitive tests available which can detect the first presence of hCG eight to nine days after conception or about four days before your expected period would come (if you weren't pregnant). The closer you get to the time of your (missed) period, the more accurate the result, because there's more hCG to pick up.

People undergoing assisted conception may be given tests to carry out at home as part of their treatment. They will receive advice on when to test – if you've had ovulation triggered by an injection of hCG, this might interfere with an accurate result in very early pregnancy. Be guided by the advice of your clinic or doctor.

Case study – Laura

I'm the sort of person who can't bear not knowing, so each time I was pregnant I did a test on the very day I would have otherwise had a period. Because of the miscarriages, this was nerve-wracking, as I wanted to be pregnant but I was afraid of losing the baby as well – but I still wanted to know as soon as possible.

There is no late limit to the use of pregnancy tests, though it's usually pointless to test as time goes on, as you will have other, obvious signs of pregnancy, like the continuing missed periods (though it is possible to continue to have sporadic bleeding in pregnancy).

FIGURING OUT THE RIGHT TIME

You need to be aware of the timing and the length of your cycle, and to be aware if you're regular or not. If you have irregular cycles, assume the cycle you are testing in is the same length as the longest you have recently experienced.

If for some reason you have lost track, you can test a minimum of 19 days after the last time you had unprotected sex, according to one of the manufacturers.

Reliability

Used properly and at the right time, home pregnancy tests are very reliable indeed. Manufacturers of the sensitive tests point out that using one four days before your missed period is less accurate than using it later – you can get a 'false negative' even if you are actually pregnant.

You can test again later in your cycle. A false negative is unlikely if you leave testing for a few more days, though you should check the instructions in the pack to be sure of the recommendations and guidance.

Sometimes, you can get a false positive – a result that says you are pregnant when you are not. This can happen with some conditions such as ovarian cysts, or the menopause – any condition where your hormones might not be as they should. If you have recently miscarried, you may also test positive for some weeks.

There are ways to use the test incorrectly:

▶ *you may test too soon*
▶ *you may fail to put the urine in the right place or for long enough*
▶ *you may use an out-of-date test*
▶ *you may be looking too soon for a result – it can take a few minutes to process.*

Generally speaking though, all the modern tests are easy to use correctly, and if you have not miscarried, if you don't suspect an underlying hormonal disorder and you don't test too soon, you can rely on the test. Manufacturers claim a higher than 99 per cent accuracy rate, not just in the lab but also in use by consumers.

Insight

A pregnancy test will give you a very reliable result immediately. If it says you are not pregnant, test again a day or so later if your period still doesn't arrive. It's possible (though unlikely) that the test is wrong.

Remember!

Ordinary medications, including the contraceptive pill, do not affect the result.

To support accuracy even more, you can test with the first urine of the day, which will have the hCG in its most concentrated form. But this isn't necessary except when you are testing early – enough hCG will be present at whatever time of day you're testing if you're using the kit a few days later. It's fine to take it to work, if you don't want to do it at home, or haven't time (it usually takes 2–10 minutes for the test to develop). It's sensible not to drink too much fluid before you test, as this can dilute the urine and make it harder for the test to pick up the hCG.

Case study – Rowena

I bought the cheapest test I could from the chemist and it was negative! I waited a week and did another one and it was positive. I knew already though, without testing. I did take a bottle of wee to my GP and she laughed... apparently you don't do that anymore, they just believe you.

A POSITIVE, THEN A NEGATIVE... OR A PERIOD?

If you have a positive result, then you're almost certainly pregnant. If you then have a negative result or a period, maybe a few days later than normal, you could have had an early miscarriage. Early pregnancy loss is very common.

Other ways of confirming pregnancy

Pregnancy can be confirmed by ultrasound, from about four weeks after conception (that is, six weeks pregnant). This is not often done, and the technique is normally used if there's some doubt about whether or not you've miscarried, or if an ectopic pregnancy is suspected after a confirmed pregnancy. A transvaginal ultrasound is likely to be done in these cases, especially as it's more sensitive at detecting an ectopic pregnancy than the abdominal ultrasound, which is more common as a part of antenatal care.

A 'dating' scan may be done at about 12 weeks, but this is not to confirm pregnancy, but to help confirm when your baby is due. It will be an abdominal scan.

It's possible to confirm a pregnancy by doing a vaginal examination and observing the cervix and feeling the uterus from the outside, but this would hardly ever be done these days – it's not necessary and could possibly be a risky interference with the pregnancy. It might also rupture an ectopic pregnancy.

If for some reason you haven't had a pregnancy test and you present for care later in pregnancy, the midwife or doctor can check if you're pregnant by palpation – feeling the uterus from the outside and checking how high in the abdominal cavity it is, to estimate the length of your pregnancy. From 18–22 weeks, you can feel the baby move – but by that time, you will have a rounded tummy and will definitely 'show', at least without clothing.

Case study – Suki

Waiting to see if I was pregnant was no problem, as I felt confident that I just wouldn't be. I'd got used to it, in a way. The pregnancy was confirmed with a blood test at the fertility clinic – I felt that pee sticks would be cheating (I don't know why). The few weeks after initial diagnosis, before the first scan, were excruciating and punctuated by light bleeding, so again, I felt everything was going wrong.

It's also possible to confirm a pregnancy with a blood test, but this is not done at home. The test looks for hCG in the same way as a urine test.

Other signs of early pregnancy which are more subjective and which can't be tested for include:

- *feeling sick and sometimes being sick*
- *changes to the breasts – you may feel they are more sensitive, experience a tingling, or notice the small glands (Montgomery's tubercles) on the nipple becoming more prominent*
- *increased need to urinate*
- *increased fatigue*
- *unfamiliar taste in the mouth.*

Some women say they 'feel' pregnant – they just know they are. It may be a combination of the symptoms on the list, or just a form of intuition.

Case study – Flo

I knew the day I conceived (my partner didn't believe me though) – we'd had sex when the monitor said* and the next day I went to London. I fainted on the tube and I just knew. Then a couple of weeks later, I was a day late with my period, and felt really ropey and slept all day – I was really certain by then.

*See p. 54 for more information on fertility monitors.

Insight

See your doctor or midwife once you are sure you are pregnant. There's no immediate rush however, unless you know you have health problems. The doctor or midwife will arrange your antenatal care, including offering any screening tests.

THINGS TO REMEMBER

1 *All pregnancy tests work in the same way every time, by measuring the presence of a hormone called hCG in your urine.*

2 *The main function of hCG in early pregnancy is to maintain the corpus luteum, stimulating its production of the hormone progesterone, which in turn supports the pregnancy.*

3 *Standard tests for home use are sensitive enough to react to hCG two weeks or so after conception, on the day you miss your period.*

4 *Accuracy is more than 99 per cent, if used correctly.*

5 *Pregnancy can be confirmed by ultrasound from about four weeks after conception.*

6 *Other signs of early pregnancy include feeling sick, and sometimes actually being sick.*

7 *Breasts can feel more sensitive in early pregnancy.*

8 *Some women feel they are pregnant without actually having any signs.*

10

Good health in early pregnancy

In this chapter you will learn:
- *about the diagnostic and screening tests on offer in early pregnancy*
- *how best to cope with sickness*
- *about foods you are advised to avoid in pregnancy.*

If you've had a difficult time trying to get pregnant, or some disappointing and saddening times on your journey, you may feel a lot of pressure from within yourself – and sometimes perhaps others – to care for your health very consciously and protectively, especially in the early weeks. Sometimes, you may not feel especially healthy – you may feel sick, tired and stressed. But don't despair, there are ways to help you cope better, and many things you can do to help make the first months more enjoyable and manageable.

First antenatal appointment

At some point in the first trimester – the first third, or first three months of pregnancy – your antenatal care will begin. You'll be offered a number of tests, either screening tests or diagnostic tests.

▶ *Screening tests are done to select which women may gain some benefit from further investigations. They don't diagnose* a condition, but allow you and your carers to assess the risk of having a baby with a particular condition, or of having something yourself (an example would be high blood pressure).

▶ Diagnostic tests are more specific, as the name implies. No test is 100 per cent accurate, and it's sensible to ask about the possibility of false negatives and false positives. These tests are often offered to women who have been assessed as already being at a greater risk of something (for example, Down's syndrome, because of being older), or because of the result of the screening test.

Your antenatal care begins with the booking appointment. This is done with a midwife. The aim is to get down on paper all your basic health information, your pregnancy history and your fertility story, plus information like the possibility of inherited conditions, any health problems you have experienced in this pregnancy so far, and also to outline what you can expect from the rest of your antenatal care.

You can use this appointment to discuss any preferences you have about the type of birth you want, and where you want to have your baby. The 'booking' part of the appointment alerts the system to your due date and allows the maternity services to expect you around about then. If you plan a home birth, now's the time to talk about it, but nothing you decide at this point is set in stone, you can change your mind at any time.

It's during this appointment that you'll probably hear from the midwife's information about future screening tests, about healthy nutrition, and about anything you need to know about your work and any hazards associated with it, if you haven't yet discussed it.

Insight

You can change your mind about where you have your baby at any time during your pregnancy. However, it makes sense to discuss your options soon enough for your carers to make the right arrangements.

FIRST ULTRASOUND SCAN

This is known as the 'dating scan', and it's usually offered between eight and 13 weeks, even when you're sure you know when you conceived. Accuracy is good, and they can estimate conception to within a few days – though this doesn't mean you know for sure the date your baby will be born, as this is very variable. Full term babies are born at any time between 38 and 42 weeks.

The scan will pick up twins (or more), too.

The sonographer takes some measurements:

▶ *the length of the foetus' torso*
▶ *the diameter of the cranium*
▶ *the length of the thigh bone.*

These all give an accurate assessment of the length of your pregnancy and act as a useful baseline for further comparative measurements taken later in your pregnancy.

It's also possible to see some serious limb or organ abnormalities at this stage.

Tests

BLOOD TESTS

Routine blood tests (all on the same blood sample) ascertain your blood group, including whether you are Rhesus positive or negative, and your 'blood count', which means measuring your haemoglobin (red blood cells) levels for anaemia. Anaemia is a potentially serious but treatable condition in pregnancy which could affect your health, your energy levels, and the risk of haemorrhage at the birth. It also looks for evidence of some illnesses and infections such as hepatitis, syphilis, and checks that you are immune to rubella, which if caught in pregnancy can affect the development of the foetus and lead to some serious disabilities.

What's the Rhesus factor?

This is a protein on the surface of every red blood cell. Most people (up to 95 per cent) are Rhesus positive. The Rhesus factor is only ever significant if you are Rhesus negative and your baby's father is Rhesus positive, *and* if your baby has inherited the positive factor from him (your baby could be Rhesus negative like you, in which case, no problem). If your baby is Rhesus positive, your own blood could produce anti-bodies to 'fight' the blood of your baby. These antibodies may cross the placenta and damage the red blood cells of your baby.

In a first pregnancy, this is not normally an issue, but in a second or subsequent pregnancy it can present a serious danger for the baby.

The situation is monitored by regular blood checks, and you may be given Anti-D immunoglobulin injections to counter the effect as a preventative measure.

OTHER TESTS

You may be offered a blood test and a specialized scan called a nuchal translucency test to screen for Down's syndrome and other chromosomal disorders. This is a specialized ultrasound scan of the foetus' nape of the neck, done at some time between 11 and 14 weeks. The amount of fluid collected at the nape can be assessed, and if there's more than there would normally be, it can be a marker for Down's syndrome.

The risk of Down's syndrome is calculated by factoring in your age to the result – older mothers (over the age of 35 at the time of birth) are already at a higher risk of having a baby with Down's.

In addition, some biochemical markers in the blood can be elevated if the foetus has Down's. All the information – nuchal translucency, age, blood test – can be put together to calculate a risk. If the risk is high, you can then be offered a diagnostic test; this would normally be amniocentesis – from about 16 weeks of pregnancy, or chorionic villus sampling (CVS) at about 13 weeks. Both of these are invasive tests and carry a small risk of miscarriage. Screening is done first, so that only those mothers whose screening tests indicate a need for further investigations would be offered CVS or amniocentesis.

CVS and amniocentesis can also test for sickle cell anaemia and thalassaemia. These are both potentially serious blood disorders, prevalent in some ethnic groups.

Nuchal translucency is also used in some centres to assess the risk of a heart defect. This would then be followed up with a more detailed foetal echocardiogram.

Other checks offered in early pregnancy include:

- **Weight and height check.** *Being significantly over or underweight can indicate a risk of problems later on. In most cases, you won't be measured again – it's not been shown to have any clinical value as a routine measurement.*
- **Blood pressure.** *This is normally carried out at every antenatal appointment. A rise in blood pressure can indicate issues with your health and the well-being of your baby.*

You don't have to have any of these checks or screening tests. If you are not comfortable with having them, you can discuss whether you need or want them, and no one can force you. None are in any way painful, though amniocentesis and CVS will be done with a local anaesthetic – it's just that some women prefer to avoid intervention of all types in their pregnancy.

You can see what the current advice is to healthcare providers about antenatal testing by reading the National Institute for Health and Clinical Excellence (NICE)'s guidelines on their website (www.nice.org.uk).

> **Insight**
> No tests are compulsory. In addition, some tests may not
> be available in your area, or offered at the same time as in
> neighbouring areas.

How you'll feel

Feeling nauseous and sometimes actually vomiting is so common, it's actually a recognized sign of pregnancy. The traditional term is 'morning sickness', but it can happen at any time of the day. Morning is the most common time, and you can sometimes stave off the vomiting by having something to drink and a light, easily digested snack such as toast or a cracker.

There's a lot we don't know about pregnancy sickness, but it seems that it's the body's reaction to pregnancy hormones for some reason. Most women find the sickness eases off before three months at the latest (though a few unlucky women find it goes on all the way through).

Case study – Gill

In early pregnancy, I started to feel bloated and tender right away, even before I knew for sure I was pregnant. The sickness started at nine weeks and continued throughout. I felt very tired from about that point and waited in vain for the much vaunted 'energy burst' in the second trimester. The early stages were a bit of an emotional rollercoaster – the whole thing was fuelled in part by the additional hormones from the fertility treatment and a bit of my own suspended disbelief. It took ages to feel that I really was pregnant, despite all the signs.

There are a number of ways you can help yourself:

▶ *keep meals small, and make sure you have something to eat or drink every hour or so, so there's always something in your stomach*

132

> - *savoury snacks seem to be better than sweet ones for keeping nausea under control*
> - *try ginger tea – it's a traditional remedy for nausea and it's safe in pregnancy*
> - *find out what works for you and what makes your nausea worse, by keeping a food and drink diary.*

Extreme pregnancy sickness, or hyperemesis gravidarum, is rare. If you're unable to live a normal life, or find you can keep nothing down, see your doctor or midwife. Hospital treatment might be needed. Amazingly enough, even sickness as severe as this is not going to harm or deprive your baby in any way. You're just as likely as the next woman to have a healthy baby.

Sickness even seems to be connected with a lessened risk of miscarriage. The women who are sick in pregnancy tend not to miscarry (though you can't predict miscarriage precisely in this way).

Case study – Annie

We were very organized, and decided to take a holiday in early spring, knowing that if we left it until the summer, I'd be in late pregnancy and things might have got difficult and uncomfortable. What I didn't anticipate was the sickness I had – we were away for two weeks, and I was sick all day, every day.

Case study – Rowena

I didn't feel good at all... I wanted the weeks to go by and I was counting them down to the magic three months when I felt the risk of losing the baby was passed. I remember telling people that early pregnancy felt like really severe jet lag. I was disorientated and nauseous – it's as if you're not really inside your body. I struggled with having a clear mind too – writing reports and presenting were difficult, as I couldn't find the words for anything. I guess it's the hormones and also, in our case, the shock.

Case study – Marion

I felt very worried for the first 14 weeks, as I'd miscarried first time round at that time. I was hoping for symptoms to sort of 'prove' I was pregnant. It was a relief from some of the worry when I started to feel queasy at seven weeks. I was very strict about following what not to eat during pregnancy. The hardest was quitting soft cheese.

Insight

There's some evidence that multiple pregnancy leads to more pregnancy sickness – more hormones, more nausea.

Staying healthy

You can continue any positive changes you made before becoming pregnant. So:

▸ *avoid smoking or smoky atmospheres*
▸ *restrict drinking (see Chapter 6 for more details on this)*
▸ *continue taking folic acid supplements until at least 12 weeks of pregnancy*
▸ *exercise and eat well. Your midwife or doctor will be able to give you more specific information, if you're concerned about the type of exercise to do.*

Insight

Continue with folic acid supplements for the first three months of pregnancy at least.

In addition, check out the rules of safe eating in pregnancy, and ensure you have any new guidance from the midwife (you should get some written information at your booking appointment, though that's rather later than needed).

You need to avoid certain foods in pregnancy, because of the risk of food-borne pathogens that could affect you or your baby.

Listeria or listeriosis (infection by the listeria bacteria) may make you slightly unwell, but if it passes from you to your baby it can have potentially serious effects, causing miscarriage, pre-term labour or stillbirth. Avoid the following:

▶ *cook-chill foods*
▶ *soft, ripened cheese like Brie or Camembert*
▶ *unpasteurized cheese*
▶ *blue-veined cheese*
▶ *untreated milk*
▶ *pâtés.*

Listeria is very rare – it affects only one pregnant woman in 30,000 – so there is no need to be concerned if you inadvertently eat some of these foods. Just do your best to avoid them.

Q&A

Peanuts and pregnancy

Q. I've heard different opinions on this. We're trying for a baby. Should I avoid peanuts so I'm peanut-free as soon as I become pregnant?

A. The idea behind the question is that peanut allergy begins in pregnancy, and so women should avoid eating peanuts so they don't sensitize the unborn baby.

There's not a lot of research to back up any rules about not eating peanuts, but some speculation centres on people who already have a peanut allergy themselves – or rather their partner's, as the allergic woman would not be eating peanuts anyway – or who have a definite allergic condition. It's thought that if women in these susceptible groups avoid eating peanuts throughout pregnancy and breastfeeding, they might prevent this tendency being inherited by their unborn baby.

(Contd)

Peanut allergy is unpleasant, awkward and dangerous, but it's also very rare, and its causes are not well understood. To take prevention seriously though, it's understandable to wonder if you would need to avoid peanuts, plus any oils or foods that contain them, before you knew for certain you were pregnant. However, the sensitization takes place across the placenta, which is not nourishing the foetus even in its chorion form for at least a couple of weeks after conception. In August 2009, the UK government issued new advice about eating peanuts during pregnancy. It really seems the evidence is there is no need for concern – even if there is allergy in the family already: 'there is no clear evidence that eating or not eating peanuts (or foods containig peanuts) during pregnancy, whilst breast feeding or during early infant life influences the chances of a child developing a peanut allergy.' So go ahead!

Salmonella won't affect your baby if you fall ill with this form of food poisoning, but you're more likely to be seriously affected than at other times (because your immune system changes in pregnancy). Thorough cooking of poultry kills salmonella, and you should avoid raw egg. If you want to be really careful, you should only have hard boiled or well-poached eggs.

In addition, it's sensible to be aware of the risk of **toxoplasmosis**. This is caused by a small parasite which lives in soil and in cat faeces. You can guard against it by wearing gloves when handling soil, making sure you wash your hands after handling raw meat, and by avoiding touching cat litter. In fact, there seems to be virtually no risk from cats according to recent research, and if you are a cat owner, you are almost certainly immune to it. Again, toxoplasmosis is very rare, with only a few cases every year.

Insight

Inadvertent consumption of foods on the 'avoid' list is inevitable – you might forget, or not know what's in your food. It's not worth stressing about... Really.

Remember!

Let your dentist know you're pregnant if you're undergoing any treatment, such as X-rays. Your doctor needs to know too, or be reminded, if you need to take any medication. The same applies to the chemist – if you take any over-the-counter remedies, check they are safe to take.

The risk of any harm from anything like this is however very small indeed.

In the press – Pregnant with girl or boy? At-home test may tell you

Expecting mums can determine whether they're carrying a boy or a girl as early as ten weeks after conception, according to makers of an over-the-counter gender prediction test.

With IntelliGender's home gender prediction test, a urine specimen turns orange if it's a girl, green if it's a boy.

'Most parents have a great degree of curiosity to find out if they're having a boy or a girl, and it can be so excruciating to wait until the 20-week sonogram to find out,' IntelliGender co-founder Rebecca Griffin said. 'But the test was never meant to be a diagnostic tool. We don't claim 100 percent accuracy.'

The gender predictor test boasts a 78 to 80 percent accuracy rate, according to the latest IntelliGender report.

CNN, 9 June 2009

THINGS TO REMEMBER

1 *Antenatal care begins after the first few weeks of pregnancy.*

2 *You will be offered a range of screening tests and diagnostic tests.*

3 *The first routine scan is usually at about 12 weeks.*

4 *You'll be asked where you want to have your baby, but you can change your mind later on.*

5 *Most people have Rhesus positive blood; those who are Rhesus negative may need extra blood checks.*

6 *Some tests carry risks to the foetus.*

7 *Simple home remedies can help with pregnancy sickness.*

8 *Check our guidance on safe eating and drinking.*

9 *Food hygiene is important in pregnancy.*

10 *Your dentist needs to know you are pregnant if you are undergoing treatment.*

11

....

'I'm pregnant' – who to tell? And when?

In this chapter you will learn:
- *about the emotional and practical challenges to sharing the news*
- *about issues which might affect your timing*
- *about coping with adverse or critical responses.*

There are a number of practical and personal elements to the decision of who to tell, how to tell, and when to tell about your pregnancy, and individual experiences are bound to be unique. Sometimes, people's reactions to your news will surprise you, and sometimes, your own feelings about your pregnancy will guide your choices.

Telling family and friends

It's an odd thing in the twenty-first century, but a few newly pregnant women and their partners say the biggest hurdle is telling their parents about the pregnancy – it's a very public admission you've been having sex, for a start, and if you've come from a family where 'private' things have been kept private, this can be a tad uncomfortable all round, if only for a short time. However, most parents are delighted to hear they're about to become grandparents, especially if they've known either officially or unofficially you have been 'trying' for a baby.

There may be other reasons why you put off telling parents and in-laws, though. Perhaps you want to keep the pregnancy a secret between the two of you, something you can enjoy keeping as a couple. Perhaps you have parents that tend to 'muscle in' on your lives, and retaining your privacy gives you some control over how much you indicate their involvement is welcome.

Case study – Marion

Both our families were quite excited at the news. My husband wanted to wait and to keep it to ourselves, but I felt differently.

When I told my mum, she beamed, all excited and she said: 'Oh, I'm expecting a baby!' I really disliked this reaction, which I felt was taking away from me my ownership of my pregnancy. I also looked at her, for a moment actually wondering if she was pregnant herself, as well!

Case study – Rowena

I didn't want to tell anyone. I was dreading the fuss and excitement of the grandparents – they have a tendency to go over the top. It was the first grandchild for my parents, and the seventh for the in-laws. I just wanted to stave off their involvement.

The first people I told were my business partners as it would have an impact on them. I told them at just two months, as I happened to be with both of them at the same time which wasn't going to happen again for several months. I could hide it quite well as I was at home most of the time and could sleep and rest whenever I wanted.

In the end, I told my parents at about ten weeks as we were visiting them for a week and I was feeling very rough, not to mention not drinking. They would have probably thought I was seriously ill if I hadn't come clean, so I felt then was the only moment I could do it. I refused to talk about it much though, and forbade them from getting excited until three months.

I told in-laws about a month later, and then all our friends at our annual summer party at about four months.

What really helped me stay private and yet share was logging onto an online birth club. I posted there from being a few weeks pregnant, and it was great to share those early weeks with strangers who were also expecting babies in the same month.

Other family and close friends may be facing their own personal issues with fertility that make you hesitant about sharing your news straight away. It's hard for some people going through fertility treatment or with a history of miscarriage, or with few hopes of having a baby of their own, to accept the news that other people are pregnant – of course that should not have any impact on your own right to enjoy your anticipation and to share your delight, but it does throw up issues of sensitivity and timing.

Case study – Ros

One of my best friends burst into tears, which I didn't think that much of at the time. But within a few months she was pregnant too, so I guess she had been trying as well (we'd never discussed having children).

Your own experiences and worries might make you wary of sharing news too soon. Miscarriage is common (see Chapter 12), and everyone who knows your news will also know if your pregnancy ends. That may be OK, of course, as you may not want to hide it from anyone, but you may want to keep your sadness to yourselves as well, without the whole world at work and at home wondering what to say to you. Most miscarriages happen in the first 12 weeks, though this is a long time to keep the news (especially if you have known from the very earliest days, as most of us do now, with today's super-sensitive home pregnancy tests).

If you have had a previous miscarriage, more than one, or even several, the 'watchful waiting' time can be agony in itself, without feeling that the rest of the world is waiting for a repeat of the bad news. The same feeling can be there after a cycle of assisted conception – most cycles don't end in a successful pregnancy, after all. Some women wait, and in the case of previous pregnancy loss, they wait until after the time of the previous loss before sharing.

Case study – Laura

I had had three miscarriages, and the fourth time I was pregnant, I didn't tell anyone until well over three months. I'd had the experience of people knowing early on, and then having to tell them I'd lost the baby and I didn't want that to happen again. Once, someone from work came up to me in the pub, all happy, and said: 'Oh, congratulations – it's great news!' and I had lost the baby a few days before. So I had to tell her, and she felt awful and so did I. I didn't make that mistake again.

Q&A

Scared of sharing the news

Q. I lost a baby last year, and this was after two years of trying. I told everyone as soon as I knew I was pregnant, and now I wish I hadn't. People have asked me ever since 'Are you going to try again?' I've just found out I'm pregnant for the second time. What should I do this time round? I'm scared I will lose the baby once more.

A. You're probably imagining the pleased smiles and congratulations, while not quite being able to share in them – and yet understandably you want to keep these doubts and misgivings to yourself. If people ask you about whether you are trying again, can you imagine saying something like: 'Well, thanks for asking, but it's all a secret at the moment' and let them wonder what the 'it' and the 'secret' actually are. It should keep people quiet until you feel comfortable, and pregnant 'enough' to share the news.

If you've been trying to get pregnant for some time, it's not unusual to feel that sharing too soon is 'tempting fate' – pure superstition of course, but not taking anything for granted is an understandable response. It's not a failure to acknowledge or accept the pregnancy, so much as a fear it might not end up with a baby. It's a bit like the caution that prevents couples buying stuff for the baby until the last few weeks. The pushchair, the clothes and the nappies can seem like scary things to buy, when you feel you daren't show confidence in the fact that you're having a baby until he or she is actually with you on the 'outside'.

Case study – Ann

We left it for a good three months before we told anyone, even though we found out immediately. I really did want to tell someone though – so when I went with my husband to the chiropodist the day after the positive test, I found myself telling her! I had to let it out somehow.

Case study – Heather

We decided to keep it a secret for a few months, but then my mother-in-law was at our house one day when I was out, and the midwife called unexpectedly as I had asked for a home birth and she wanted to check me out! Why she couldn't have made an appointment, I don't know. Anyway, we had to tell her then – there's only one reason why the midwife calls, and that's if there's a pregnant woman in the house. My mother-in-law tried very hard not to be cross for not being told straight away!

Insight
Make sure you and your partner agree who to tell about your pregnancy and when.

Informing your employers

Employment and maternity benefits will depend on you sharing the news with your employer at some stage, naturally enough.

The legislation on this is fast changing and while large companies can be expected to have HR departments that know what your rights are, you can't be totally sure they don't make mistakes. Small companies might need their hands holding, even if you're not the first pregnant employee they've had. It will help if you inform yourself of what your pregnancy means in terms of pay, leave and the options for your return.

In the UK, you can get good information at the government's direct.gov website (www.direct.gov.uk – search on pregnancy and maternity rights). Your union or professional organization should also be able to help.

You need to let your employer know about antenatal appointments and antenatal classes you will attend (which you are entitled to go to, without loss of pay).

If you work in a job where there may be hazards to your health or your baby's health, either in the nature of the job or in the environment you're in, your employer has to allow you to change your tasks or routines, or your workplace, to somewhere safe, without any loss of pay or status.

Check the legislation for the timings. You need to know when to give notice of your intention to return to work, if this is your plan, within a time frame. It's the same for your partner. Paternity leave has to be applied for well in advance. If you give your employer(s) notice within the correct time frame, and your baby arrives pre-term, you will not be penalized for this.

Case study – Caroline

There was no real issue about whether to tell people or not –
I showed by my increased weight and change in shape almost
immediately, so it was difficult to avoid people noticing – my boss
actually asked me when I was only 6–8 weeks pregnant. I usually
wore tailored suits, and suddenly, there I was dressed in a smock!
Also, I was as sick as a dog, and I couldn't hide that.

Case study – Gill

The first time I was pregnant we were so thrilled after the long
years of trying, we told the world, all family and friends and
everyone at work. It made it much harder when we lost the baby
at such an early stage. The second time we told no one, until after
the nuchal scan – then we told our bosses, but asked them to keep
it confidential. We didn't even tell parents and close friends until
after 26 weeks (we were super-paranoid).

Insight

Don't assume that your workplace will know to keep your
pregnancy confidential, unless you ask them to.

Coping with others' reactions

Having a baby is received as good news in almost every case.
Occasionally, you may have a negative reaction from someone –
usually connected with their own personal situation. Or perhaps,
like Anne's father (below), they reveal expectations or assumptions
you didn't know they had. If there's some bad feeling towards your
partner, you might find this comes out when you share your news –
having a baby with someone is a permanent bond, whatever happens
in the future, and that can seem like a blow if there are friends or
family who would rather you split up and found another partner!

There's no easy answer to any of this, except to point out that in fact, babies can so often heal rifts and soothe troubled hearts, so the outlook is good.

Tricky relationships with in-laws can improve when you have a wonderful grandchild to share with them. The sister, sister-in-law, or the close friend who is battling with her own desires for a baby and can't bring herself to say 'congratulations', may turn out to be a terrific auntie. Don't burn your bridges with the ones who seem jealous or resentful. Things may turn out just fine.

Insight

Being sensitive to others' hopes and fears around pregnancy and birth, and their bad memories, is important.

Case study – Anne

I was taken aback by my father's reaction. I had stopped work because of redundancy and hadn't looked for another job straight away, and he said immediately: 'Is that why you stopped working?', which was just not the case. There was part of him that felt I was wasting my education, I think, but he soon came round, and he was as pleased as everyone else. I will always remember that reaction though, and how I felt on hearing it.

Case study – Paula

My father was somewhat surprised, but happy I think. My boyfriend's father was told just before a rugby cup final game and he now says watching rugby always reminds him of that time – he was most surprised.

Both my boyfriend and I lost our mothers in 1999 and we both felt that loss even more keenly around this time, as well as just after the birth.

All of our friends were very surprised, since we were only the third couple to have a child within our group of friends and we had only been together for just over a year. Telling people was strange, since it's not an easy thing to slip into conversation. However, I could not really keep it a secret, because I had also said the only thing that would stop me smoking was being pregnant, and so most people would have guessed sooner rather than later just by seeing me not have a cigarette in my hand.

We also decided to tell quite a few people before three months because we felt if anything did go wrong we would like to have the support of close friends, especially since we weren't living near each other at the time because of work commitments.

I told my other female colleagues during a meal. They were very excited. Then exactly one week later, I miscarried, and felt bad about having to tell everyone the news.

Insight

If telling people makes them share stories about their own (maybe scary) experiences and you don't want to know, you might have to politely explain you'd prefer not to hear them!

THINGS TO REMEMBER

1 *You need to think carefully about when to share the news of your pregnancy.*

2 *It's normal to be wary of sharing news too soon.*

3 *It's important to show sensitivity to others who may be experiencing fertility problems.*

4 *Antenatal care and antenatal classes can be taken as paid-for time off work.*

5 *You are entitled to a safe working environment without loss of pay or status.*

6 *You need to inform yourself about pay and benefits, and to check legislation on employment issues.*

12

Pregnancy loss: miscarriage, stillbirth, neonatal death

In this chapter you will learn:
- *about why a pregnancy might end in miscarriage*
- *about factors involved in stillbirth or death soon after birth*
- *about the emotional impact of pregnancy loss on you and your partner.*

Miscarriage, also known as spontaneous pregnancy loss, means the ending of your pregnancy. Some pregnancies also end in deliberate termination because of abnormality. Babies may also be born too soon or too ill or disabled to survive outside the uterus; others may die shortly before birth, which is known as a stillbirth.

In all these cases, the pregnancy has been wanted, even longed for, and the loss can be something that has emotional as well as physical effects, even when the loss has happened very early after conception.

The fact is that pregnancy loss can happen to anyone, at any time. It happens to healthy parents, it happens to people who take extra care with their pregnancy preparations, and to people where there is no history of miscarriage in the family. There's no reason to expect it will happen to you – and no reason to fear it, as most pregnancies progress happily and healthily.

Sometimes, there's a clear reason why a pregnancy comes to an end. Far more usually, there isn't – and as people say sometimes,

'It's one of those things', meaning it's something unpredictable, over which you have little or no control.

Statistics on the incidence of miscarriage can vary, but Tommy's charity (see Taking it further) state that one in four women experience miscarriage, and that one in five pregnancies end in miscarriage. Other sets of figures with rather different incidences are not hard to find, however. You might read that less than half of all fertilized eggs develop into a pregnancy – the fertilized egg does not implant into the uterus, almost always because there is some degree of anomaly, and nature takes its course as a result. This high rate of non-implantation shows how selective nature can be – and early miscarriage, in particular, is part of this.

Today, we tend to hear more about miscarriage, especially since it became possible to buy a cheap home pregnancy test (see Chapter 9). It's become normal to know you're pregnant only about two weeks after fertilization of the egg – on the day or the day after your period would have been due. Some tests can detect pregnancy hormone even sooner than this.

The result is that prospective parents end up knowing about pregnancies they might not otherwise have been aware of – at least, not with any certainty. In years gone by, very early pregnancy loss might not have been recognized in the physical sense as anything but a heavy and/or rather late period (which is what an early miscarriage can feel and look like). These days, however, one of the consequences of knowing so early is that the excitement and anticipation of pregnancy is present a lot sooner than before – and the disappointment and sadness at its loss is there too.

Insight

It's very common to feel guilt when you lose a baby – wishing you had done something, or not done something, and trying to think of a link between action/inaction and your loss. But there is hardly ever any connection. Share your anxieties with your doctor or midwife and they should explain.

Why do miscarriages happen?

CHROMOSOMAL ABNORMALITY

Although the reasons why a miscarriage happens are not normally routinely investigated, it's known that the majority of them happen because there is some form of genetic abnormality in the embryo or foetus. Research shows that about half of all early miscarriages (the ones before 13 weeks) show a chromosomal abnormality – not one that is inherited in any way, but one that's just happened by chance.

Usually, because it's not inherited from either parent, the chromosomal abnormality will not happen again in a future conception, and the majority of women go on to have a normal, full-term pregnancy the next time round. However, in contrast to this, there are some repeated chromosomal problems that can be caused by either you or your partner passing on an abnormality, and this would be one of the aspects tested if you continued to miscarry. This issue affects between three and five per cent of couples experiencing recurrent miscarriage, according to guidelines from the Royal College of Obstetricians and Gynaecologists.

BIOCHEMICAL/HORMONAL FACTORS

When a woman's hormones (the chemical 'messengers' in her body) circulate to encourage one part of the body to 'do something' or not, as the case may be, high or low levels of a particular hormone or collection of hormones can prevent the body from nurturing a developing pregnancy. The result is the pregnancy is then lost.

Conditions in this category that increase the risk of miscarriage include polycystic ovaries, which are cysts on the ovaries produced by unusually high levels of a hormone known as LH (luteinizing hormone) plus high levels of the hormone testosterone. Some treatments adjust the level of hormones in the body, to make the body more likely to produce the right biochemical environment for the pregnancy.

PROBLEMS WITH YOUR UTERUS OR CERVIX

If you have a cervix that stretches and opens too soon – sometimes termed an 'incompetent cervix' in some studies (not the most supportive phrasing) – you are at risk of a late miscarriage. Everything is OK until maybe 16–20 weeks of pregnancy, when the cervix starts to struggle to remain closed. Cervical cerclage, a stitch inserted into the cervix, can help (though exactly which women will benefit from this is the subject of an ongoing study – we don't yet know precisely who should have this treatment).

Some women have a uterus that's an unusual shape, preventing the normal growth of the foetus, and leading to miscarriage. Or perhaps the structural difficulty is a divided uterus – there are two compartments in the uterus, divided by the thin tissue which effectively cuts off the available space.

Pre-existing fibroids might also make it hard for the uterus to make room for the baby.

BLOOD-CLOTTING DISORDERS

There are several disorders, including some auto-immune conditions, such as Hughes Syndrome, also known as antiphospholipid syndrome, that lead to a problem with blood clotting; you may not know you have it, as it can be symptom-free. Blood needs to flow freely and normally, and blood which is 'sticky' and clots too regularly becomes less efficient at doing its job. Women who have recurrent miscarriages may be tested for antiphospholipid syndrome.

Blood flow can affect the way the very early pregnancy is nourished by the blood, and later, how the placenta safeguards the foetus. When blood flow is reduced, the health and growth of the foetus are compromised. In serious cases, this can lead to the pregnancy miscarrying, or in later pregnancy, stillbirth.

Some women can be treated with anti-clotting medication if it's thought this condition is affecting their ability to continue with a normally developing pregnancy.

INFECTION

This covers a wide range of possible situations. Some blood infections can lead to miscarriage; food-borne infections such as listeria can cause birth defects or lead to miscarriage.

BLIGHTED OVUM

This describes the formation of a sac, developed from the fertilized egg, but with no foetus inside it. Pregnancy hormones are produced, so your periods stop and you may even feel pregnancy sickness and other symptoms, but sadly there is no developing foetus. This can cause a 'missed miscarriage' (see below). It can also be termed an 'anembryionic pregnancy', or a pregnancy without an embryo. This is most likely to happen as a matter of chance only, and subsequent pregnancies will be unaffected.

HYDATIDIFORM MOLE/MOLAR PREGNANCY

This happens when the trophoblast (which is the precursor of the placenta) grows very quickly, and becomes a mass of cells filled with fluid. It grows to fill the womb, and no embryo can develop. Sometimes there is no embryo at all, and in other cases, there is only the beginning of one. The usual pregnancy hormones are produced, but in larger amounts, and this can cause excessive sickness and nausea. There's likely to be intermittent bleeding from the uterus. Molar pregnancy is very unusual, and afterwards you will be followed up carefully, as very rarely a molar pregnancy can lead to a cancerous tumour of the chorion. Like blighted ovum, this is unlikely to occur again.

ECTOPIC PREGNANCY

This is not a miscarriage, but a pregnancy which has started to develop in the 'wrong' place, usually in one of the fallopian tubes.

First signs of an ectopic pregnancy are pain and weakness, and possibly bleeding. Ectopic pregnancy is serious if not treated, and needs surgical intervention to end the pregnancy. Most women go on to conceive and carry a subsequent pregnancy to term, though conception may take longer to occur if the functioning of the affected tube has been compromised.

OTHER CAUSES

Multiple pregnancies – twins, triplets or more – have a higher risk of miscarriage. It's hard to say the fact of being a multiple has caused the miscarriage, but it may be the uterus and/or cervix are somehow reacting to the greater strain.

Women who are significantly overweight are at higher risk of miscarriage, shown in a number of studies. The same applies to women who are significantly underweight before becoming pregnant.

Possible risk factors for miscarriage

A study in the February 2007 issue of the *British Journal of Obstetrics and Gynaecology* reports on research into risk factors for miscarriage. A UK-wide study compared 1,200 mothers, divided in two groups; one who carried their pregnancies beyond 12 weeks and one with those who lost their pregnancies before this time. The results confirmed the reason for most miscarriages is not fully understood, and supposed risk factors are still unconfirmed.

Mothers who were older, and mothers who had a history of fertility problems and previous miscarriages were more likely to miscarry.

Other factors which appeared to increase the risk were having a low body weight before pregnancy, drinking alcohol regularly or in large amounts, and feeling stressed.

In addition, a recent change of partner was a risk factor – and mothers whose partner was older were also more likely to miscarry.

In an interesting finding, the belief that pregnancy sickness is associated with a lowered risk of miscarriage was confirmed – nausea and vomiting meant an almost 70 per cent reduction in risk.

There was no connection between miscarriage and caffeine, moderate or only occasional alcohol intake and smoking; and no socio-economic or educational factors stood up to scrutiny either. Working during pregnancy was not relevant. A healthy diet appeared to lower risk.

British Journal of Obstetrics and Gynaecology, February 2007

Incidence of miscarriage

There is a rise in the incidence of miscarriage in women over 30, a sharp rise in women over 35, and a further sharp rise in women aged over 40.

Older fathers may increase the risk of miscarriage too. In studies, the age of the father was an independent factor in miscarriage, and there is a slightly higher risk of miscarriage where the father is aged more than 40.

Overall, about one pregnancy in every five ends in miscarriage, and each year, 100,000 women experience a miscarriage.

Recurrent miscarriage is usually defined as three or more consecutive miscarriages. Specialist clinics in the UK may be willing to talk to you if you have had no more than two miscarriages, but do talk this through with your doctor. Having investigations sooner is obviously more important if you're older and feel time is running out, or if you know or suspect you have an underlying health problem you think might be affecting your early pregnancy health or chances of conception.

However, the figures show that even after three miscarriages, the chance of having a successful pregnancy are still higher than having a further miscarriage. This is why medical help for recurrent miscarriage may not be offered until at least three or even four miscarriages have happened – nature has a better than 50 per cent chance of doing the job properly, without intervention (figures based on tables at www.tommys.org).

In the future, it's likely that research will investigate the man's role in recurrent miscarriage too. A paper from Wayne State University Medical School's Reproductive Endocrine and Infertility division in Detroit, Michigan, gives an overview of the situation, pointing out that there may be genetic factors, semen factors and age contributing to the problem. 'With further investigation, evaluation of the male may be considered a routine part of the evaluation in the near future.' (From *Current Opinion, Obstetrics and Gynaecology*, June 2007.)

Case study – Laura

After the first two miscarriages, when I was nine weeks and then 12 weeks, I began to think we were never going to be parents. And I was scared of becoming pregnant again, because I didn't want to go through the heartbreak of losing the baby all over again. Then when I became pregnant for a third time, and miscarried again, this time at seven weeks, I felt even worse. We were going for hospital tests when I became pregnant for the fourth time. I was terrified. When you miscarry again and again, it takes all the joy away – I could not really believe I could carry a pregnancy to the end, and actually end up with a healthy baby. It wasn't until our little daughter was finally here that I truly accepted that we would be parents.

One thing I feel strongly about is that the grief of miscarriage is not always acknowledged by other people. I hated hearing things like: 'Oh, well, it wasn't meant to be' or 'There must have been something wrong with it', or 'It's bound to happen one day'. Some people don't understand the sorrow of miscarriage is real.

How do you become aware of miscarriage?

Signs a miscarriage may be about to happen include:

▶ *pain, like a 'period pain' caused by the contractions of the uterus*
▶ *bleeding from the vagina*
▶ *leaking of the waters, the amniotic fluid that surrounds the foetus (in later miscarriage).*

Usually, these signs are followed by the loss of the foetus, with the loss of the placenta and membranes.

Sometimes, women experience a 'missed' miscarriage or 'missed abortion' – the foetus dies, and the pregnancy does not exist any longer, but the body fails to expel what doctors sometimes call 'the products of conception'. There may be a small amount of dark brown blood loss, but no other sign, and the fact the miscarriage has occurred may only show up at the routine scan. This is sometimes termed a 'delayed miscarriage'.

WHAT HAPPENS NEXT?

If you suspect you're about to have a miscarriage, because of bleeding or other symptoms, you need to speak to your doctor or midwife as soon as you can. Slight bleeding, or even heavier bleeding, that stops is very common in early pregnancy. Bed rest used to be the advice, but there's no real evidence that this does any good – a healthy, normal pregnancy will be fine with or without bed rest, and bed rest does not prevent a miscarriage. Your doctor may discuss hospital admission with you.

It may be necessary to have surgery to make sure your uterus has expelled everything. This is called 'evacuation of retained products of conception', and is done under general anaesthetic. With a late miscarriage or a stillbirth, this is not an option, and you will be given medication to start you off in labour. Alternatively, you will be given 'expectant management' – letting nature take its course without inducing labour. Your own feelings and preference should be taken into account when this decision is made.

Recovery after miscarriage

PHYSICALLY

Your physical recovery can take a few days, and it's fair to say that later miscarriages or stillbirths can take as long a recovery as you would need from a normal labour and birth.

You'll probably start your periods again after 4–6 weeks. It's normal for you to notice rather heavier bleeding than before, and for your period to last a day or so longer than you have been used to.

Speak to your doctor about your concerns if you want to explore having tests or treatment for miscarriage. If it looks like the miscarriage (or miscarriages) are 'sporadic' – occurring as 'one-offs' by chance, even if in fact there have been more than one – your doctor may discuss with you the option of simply going ahead and 'trying again'. If it appears there may be a different reason, you may be able to have tests to either confirm your miscarriages are still sporadic, or if there is some other underlying reason.

Treatment for recurrent miscarriage has made progress in recent years, though we are still a long way from being able to reassure women that as long as they can become pregnant, a safe and normal pregnancy will eventually happen, with the right miscarriage prevention.

Treatments once thought to be effective sometimes drop out of favour after a time. This isn't 'fashion' or a doctor's whim, it's usually when larger studies show treatments or interventions don't have as many positive outcomes as was once thought, or that the intervention needs to be targeted more exactly at the people most likely to be helped by it. This is not only the case with the cerclage technique (see p. 154), but it also affects drug treatment for blood disorders and hormonal treatment.

Insight

Research into possible treatments for recurrent miscarriage goes on all the time. Keep checking newspapers and the internet for news on this.

EMOTIONALLY

Your emotional response will be very individual to you. You may find yourself struggling with a range of emotions. You may have already imagined the baby you were going to have, and you may need to grieve for him or her. With a later miscarriage or stillbirth, you will also look and feel different, which in itself can be a difficult reminder of your loss.

Mothers experience the physical effects and may sometimes feel as if it's something they should blame themselves for; they can feel angry and guilty as if they have somehow let their partner down. Dads too grieve after pregnancy loss and will need time and space for their own feelings. It can be a very sad time for both of you.

Insight

If someone you know has a miscarriage, stay sensitive. It's not at all comforting for someone to hear that 'It's probably all for the best' or 'Nature knows what she's doing'.

Termination for abnormality

Antenatal care includes testing and screening for the health and development of the foetus. Occasionally, testing results in a diagnosis of serious abnormality, or a condition that would not permit the baby to survive. The sort of diagnoses involved include chromosomal abnormalities such as Down's syndrome, Edwards syndrome, or heart defects.

On these occasions, you will be offered the possibility of termination. You will be given time, and counselling, to help you decide what to do. You may need to find out more about the diagnosis, and what impact it would have on your family. You can get good information and support from ARC (see Taking it further).

Finding out from a scan or a diagnostic test that your much-wanted baby has an abnormality is deeply shocking. When it happens, people who are only just getting used to the idea of being parents find themselves in what some described as 'a parallel world' or 'nightmare' where they felt confused, dazed and sick with worry. Once they take the baby's diagnosis on board, they're then faced with the kind of decision that no one ever wants to have to make.

Dr Kate Field, DIPex – who have collected the experiences of parents, www.healthtalkonline.org

Remember!

In the UK the usual limit for termination of pregnancy is 24 weeks, but in the case of severe abnormality, there is no upper limit.

Stillbirth and neonatal death

When a baby dies in later pregnancy or very soon after birth, both you and the people around you share in the knowledge – you and those close to you have grown accustomed to looking forward to the birth, you will have felt the movement of the baby, and you may have bought clothing and equipment. All this combines to make the baby real, and for the sad loss of your baby to leave a devastating gap in your life.

Causes of stillbirth and neonatal death are many – often they are related to prematurity, when the baby is born too young to have the best chance of survival, or they are related to a disability or condition that weakens the baby's grasp on life.

This is not the book to go into detail about the causes of this type of loss. If it happens to you, you will find support from SANDS (see Taking it further). There are also local groups and telephone help.

Insight

If you experience a late miscarriage, a stillbirth or a termination for abnormality, you'll be asked if you want to see your baby. This can be very comforting. Hospital staff will respect your wishes either way, and will not pressurize you. You don't have to decide on this straight away, so take some time to think about it.

Explanation of terms

Miscarriage: loss of pregnancy before 23 weeks gestation (counted from the first day of the last menstrual period).
Neonatal death: death of an infant within 28 days of birth.
Stillbirth: when a baby is born dead after the 23rd completed week of pregnancy.
Termination for abnormality: chosen by parents after counselling, after antenatal tests have revealed a problem. Before 13 weeks, the pregnancy is ended surgically. After that time, birth is induced, and labour and delivery follow. An injection to ensure the foetus dies before birth is usually given after 18 weeks.

Our baby was beautiful. She was amazing to see. We don't know why she died – everything so far is inconclusive. The sadness is so great. It will live with me until my dying day. It's hard for fathers too. I was totally devastated, but of course I had to be there with my wife during the labour, and stay strong for her.

Ben, stillbirth at 26 weeks.

I went for my routine antenatal appointment at 39 weeks. I had felt there might be something not right, as the baby had not moved for a few days... then they couldn't find a heartbeat, and I was told my baby had died.

When I went into labour, though, I was excited. It was as if my body's normal responses kicked in. When Thomas was born, I felt delight, I felt I had achieved something. I will always be a mother.

The best thing people can say? It's just very simple – 'I'm sorry'.

Katie, stillbirth at 39 weeks.

Contributors to Jeremy Vine show, BBC Radio 2, 3 April 2007

Insight

Pregnancy loss is bad luck, in most cases. It's unusual to be able to find a definite reason for it.

Trying again

When you've suffered pregnancy loss, you may experience a range of emotions when you consider whether to become pregnant again – mothers report sometimes feeling very anxious to try again, others are sometimes scared, in case they are somehow courting disaster.

Ask your doctor about when it would be physically advisable to try to conceive again – in most cases, there's nothing to stop you trying straight away. Your next fertile time will be about two weeks after your next period.

If you have had a late miscarriage, stillbirth or neonatal death, there can be more complex emotional issues, and becoming pregnant very soon may be a confusing and upsetting time – you're grieving a real person, not the expectation or hope of one, and you may need to think about allowing yourself time and space for this. Talk to your partner and people who care for you, and reach the decision that's right for you.

Q&A

Try again – or wait?

Q. I've had two miscarriages, both fairly early. We had been trying for some years to become pregnant, so it was devastating to suffer the disappointment after the joy of discovering I was pregnant. My husband suggests we 'take six months off' trying for a baby and actively use contraception, and then think again after that time – his view is we need a break from the pressure, and if I know I definitely won't get pregnant, I can step off the rollercoaster. I don't know what to do. I fear time is running out and we should try to 'seize the day' and continue.

A. You're facing a dilemma many couples have to grapple with. There is a notion, often voiced by people who are trying to help, that you can 'try too hard to get pregnant'. There is really no scientific support for this at all, but enough couples conceive when they've decided to stop trying – but this happens almost certainly by chance rather than anything else. Some couples undergoing fertility treatment do conceive naturally, even when investigations have told them it's unlikely, and the treatment had nothing to do with it at all, or they suspend treatment for some reason, and then

(Contd)

conceive perfectly spontaneously. Perhaps this is what is in the back of your husband's mind?

Your other issue is the experience of the two miscarriages. Early loss is almost always 'sporadic' – not caused by anything but bad luck, and it's perfectly possible to have two 'bad luck' miscarriages on the trot, or even more than that. Nature isn't a bit fussy about sharing out the bad luck between different people.

Long-term fertility problems can mean life is dominated by pregnancy tests, scheduled sexual intercourse, ovulation kits and calendars, and it's easy to forget the relationship at the heart of the wish for a baby. Maybe this again is what your husband is trying to bring to the decision-making?

Your choice will come out of talking and maybe compromising – having sex without contraception but spontaneously, and not when you 'should' be having it, might be an option. You might have to agree not to keep buying pregnancy tests too!

THINGS TO REMEMBER

1 *Pregnancy loss can be a matter of chance, happening to healthy people unexpectedly.*

2 *Most pregnancy loss happens without a definite reason being found.*

3 *One in four women experience miscarriage.*

4 *Miscarriage appears to be more common in recent years because women know they are pregnant sooner than they used to.*

5 *The majority of miscarriages happen because the pregnancy was not viable in some way.*

6 *Incidence of miscarriage rises with age.*

7 *Recurrent miscarriage is defined as three or more consecutive miscarriages.*

8 *Slight bleeding or bleeding that ceases is very common in early pregnancy, and does not always mean miscarriage.*

9 *If the foetus is found to have an abnormality, you may be offered a termination.*

10 *Pregnancy loss can profoundly affect both men and women.*

13

....

What next after tests and checks?

In this chapter you will learn:
- *when surgical treatment for fertility problems may be an option*
- *about the use of pharmaceutical help*
- *about the different forms of assisted reproduction.*

We've already seen how fertility help and support involves the checking and testing described in Chapter 7. The next step may be treatment for the problems that emerge from the checking – that's if the investigations revealed anything, or anything treatable.

Sometimes, you're told there is nothing amiss – you and your partner appear to be fertile, or fertile enough to conceive and have a successful pregnancy. There may be an explanation of why it seems to be taking rather longer to have a baby, and you may be advised to make the most of the fertility you have by changing your lifestyle, making healthier decisions and scheduling sex with some fertility awareness (see Chapter 4). Beyond that, your specialist or clinic may simply suggest you continue expecting to become pregnant at some point, without any particular intervention or medical help.

It may be that one or more diagnostic investigations you have had, has carried out the treatment for you – the tests for fallopian tube patency (openness) can unblock them, if this has been a problem. Laparoscopy and other investigative tests may be diagnostic in their main aim, but the surgeon may be able to treat some observed conditions as well. Fibroids, adhesions and endometriosis can be dealt with at the same time, by removal of the tissue. If you have the condition called a hydrosalpinx, which is a build up of fluid blocking the end of the fallopian tube, this may also be treated in this way. Some specialists would recommend removal of the tubes if you have this, but this of course would mean you could not conceive without assisted reproduction.

Insight

Undergoing tests, investigations and treatment can be lonely and dispiriting. Seek help and friendship from support groups, in real life or online.

Insight

Finding out there is nothing unusual or abnormal revealed by investigations can be difficult – it may mean a decision on whether to keep on hoping or not.

Surgical help

Blocked fallopian tubes can sometimes be cleared with an operation called salpingography with tubal catheterization or cannulation. This involves the insertion of a very fine instrument into the fallopian tubes which clears them out, with the intention of allowing the egg and the sperm to travel freely.

Surgery can also remove endometriosis and adhesions in the pelvis. This can help to restore a normal menstrual cycle, including regular ovulation.

Sometimes, women with polycystic ovarian syndrome (PCOS – see Chapter 12) are offered surgery called laparoscopic ovarian drilling. It uses the laparoscopy technique to enter the pelvis (via a small incision just below your navel, just as we've seen before in Chapter 7). A heat process is then applied to different places on the ovaries, with the aim of reducing the over-active production of androgen hormones, which is thought to be one of the reasons why PCOS can interfere with fertility.

Endometriosis and fertility

Q. I've just been diagnosed with endometriosis and I've been told this is likely to be the reason for the fact I have not become pregnant. Is there any treatment for the condition?

A. Some women are unlucky enough to suffer from endometriosis for a long time, getting nowhere, and not actually getting a diagnosis for years.

Endometriosis is a condition where the cells that make up the lining of the womb grow elsewhere. They behave just as if they were in the uterus, though – reacting to hormonal changes and bleeding, which can mean pain and swelling in the abdominal cavity – the blood can't escape through the vagina, and it may lead to the formation of adhesions, which stick tissue and organs together. In its worst forms, it can affect all the organs of the pelvis causing a lot of pain. It can also lead to cysts on the ovaries, which may not cause any symptoms, but may need to be removed to avoid the chance that they burst, which can be very painful.

Endometriosis is suspected by its symptoms, and diagnosed by looking at the pelvic organs during laparoscopy. Some cases can be treated by surgical removal of the endometrial deposits, but this may not be enough for serious cases, and the endometriosis can return too. There are some hormonal treatments for endometriosis – they work as long as they are being taken, and don't act as a cure. There are side effects too, and you may need to work through different treatments and combinations of treatments to find out the one that helps you most. The most common side effects are similar to menopausal symptoms (fatigue, hot flushes, headaches), because the treatment is designed to stop you producing oestrogen.

Endometriosis can interfere with your fertility, and it's a common finding it in women who need fertility investigations. However, many women with endometriosis conceive and have trouble-free pregnancies.

Q&A

Fibroids and fertility

Q. I've been told I have fibroids. This is something my mother suffered from for many years, although it didn't stop her having children. Will it affect my fertility? I already have heavy periods which last for several days, but I haven't had any other symptoms.

A. Fibroids are benign growths or tumours which are very common – estimates are that up to one-third of women have them and sometimes even more in some ethnic groups. Only about one-quarter of all women with fibroids will have symptoms, which include, as you say, heavy periods. Their effect on fertility varies – if they are actually in the uterine cavity, they can prevent the fertilized egg implanting in the uterine wall. Some fibroids can block the fallopian tubes.

You might be able to have an examination which would show where your fibroids are and get an opinion on whether they might make it more difficult for you to conceive. Fibroids can sometimes be removed with surgery (this is called myomectomy), but it can depend on the site of them, how many and how big they are.

It's becoming more common for fibroids to be removed before IVF, as research shows IVF is likely to be more successful if this happens.

PCOS and fertility

Q. Polycystic ovarian syndrome (PCOS) has been in the news a lot. How do I know I have it, and whether it will affect my chances of pregnancy?

A. Most women with this condition don't have any problems conceiving and maintaining a pregnancy, but some can. There is a wide spectrum of symptoms, and probably most women who have a mild form of the condition don't even notice they have it.

It describes multiple tiny cysts on the ovaries, caused by many more follicles than usual beginning to develop before ovulation. They don't mature, but instead form a gradually increasing number of cysts on the ovary. This means the normal level of hormones is affected, and the body produces greater amounts of male hormone, as well as larger amounts of oestrogen.

It can also happen that you have PCOS but without the cysts – in this case it just describes the hormone imbalance.

Some women with PCOS ovulate only very irregularly, and some don't ovulate at all. Other symptoms include weight gain, excess body hair including hair on the face, thinning hair on the scalp and lack of periods. It can affect fertility, because with irregular or no ovulation, conception can't take place.

Doctors can help with some of the symptoms by prescribing hormone treatment, and there's some evidence that surgery can help. The procedure is called ovarian drilling – it destroys part of the ovary and seems to work by affecting the way the ovary's biochemistry functions, reducing hormone production. This prevents the formation of new follicles, and relieves symptoms.

If you're overweight, losing weight can help, and it can also improve fertility. It can be a difficult condition to deal with though. Research has linked PCOS with abnormalities in the blood clotting system, via a variant in a gene labelled PAI-1, which is involved both with the breakdown of blood clots and the implantation of the embryo. Fathers may also carry this variation, and this too may affect the ability to conceive and carry the pregnancy to term.

Fertility drugs

The right drugs can stimulate your body to produce and release an egg from the ovaries. If you're not ovulating regularly, or even if you appear to be and there has been no pregnancy and no explanation of why, you can be prescribed hormone drugs to stimulate the process.

Currently, the two drugs in most use for this are clomifene citrate or tamoxifen. When you take either of these, you will be monitored to see what your response is, and to try to adjust the dose to reduce the chance of a multiple pregnancy (your ovulation 'performance' can be checked by ultrasound).

There are other possible drugs to be used in addition or instead of these, and there are advances in therapies and combinations of therapies all the time – your clinic should explain to you what you are using, what the side effects might be, and the length of time they plan to prescribe it for you. Sometimes, you may find the use of drug therapy produces side effects you don't like – the symptoms are sometimes described as menopausal. You may get hot flushes, mood swings and tiredness.

Gonadotrophins, which include follicle-stimulating hormone (FSH) and luteinizing hormone (LH), are hormones produced naturally in every normal menstrual cycle. They're needed to promote ovulation and to protect and develop the egg before and after fertilization. They're available in drug form, if it's thought you may not be producing enough of your own.

Again, the way your body responds will be checked by ultrasound; too high a dose for you increases the risk of a multiple pregnancy. In addition, your ovaries may get over-stimulated, which increases the risk of developing ovarian hyperstimulation syndrome. At its worst, this means painful abdominal swelling because of an over-retention of fluid in and around the ovaries. It can result in kidney damage and thrombosis. If this happens, you will need hospital treatment and a review of your drug regime when you recover. In extreme cases, it can even be fatal.

If the tests you have undergone when you are investigated for fertility problems have revealed a disorder of the pituitary gland called hyperprolactinaemia – which is an excess of prolactin production – you can be offered specific treatment. Hyperprolactinaemia gives you an irregular menstrual cycle, and you may produce breast milk. There are drugs available for this, called dopamine agonists. You may be advised to undergo some further checks to rule out an underlying cause of the disorder, such as a pituitary tumour.

Insight
Drug treatments for fertility problems may have unpleasant side effects. Find out from your doctor what they are and how long they might be expected to last.

Treatment for men

If the checks you have had have shown problems, there are some treatment options that have been shown to be worth trying. Blockages (such as a cyst or cysts) in the testicles inhibiting sperm flow can be removed surgically.

If tests have shown you have a lower than normal amount of the hormones that stimulate sperm production, hormone treatment might be offered to boost your levels.

Some men are unable to ejaculate, usually because of previous surgery on the prostate gland, or because of a side effect of diabetes (the valve system that controls the flow of urine versus the flow of semen through the urethra stops working properly. Instead of the sperm issuing at ejaculation, they come out with the urine). Drugs that work on the neck of the bladder may help. Another way is to harvest the sperm from a sample of urine for use with assisted reproduction techniques.

If you have a low sperm count, or the sperm are seen to be poor in quality, it may be possible to retrieve sperm with a surgical process called sperm recovery, which obtains sperm direct from the testes with fine-needle aspiration. Again, this is used with assisted reproduction techniques; normally, enough would be removed to allow for freezing, so further attempts at retrieval will not be needed in the future.

Q&A

Vasectomy reversal

Q. My partner has been married before, and he has two children with his first wife. He got a vasectomy when the younger one was three, because he was sure at the time he didn't want any more children. Then his marriage broke up, and we got together. What are the chances he can have a reversal?

A. Vasectomy describes the surgical operation that severs the vas deferens leading from each testicle, so the sperm cannot reach the penis and be ejaculated with the seminal fluid (semen). When it's effective, it makes a man unable to father children – no sperm, no conception. Sperm continue to be made, but they just degenerate inside the testes and dissolve. In a very few cases, the vas spontaneously rejoins and the man becomes fertile again, but it's so rare, you can't actually hope for that happening.

A reversal means re-joining each vas, to make a continuous tube that will transport sperm as before. An alternative method is to
(Contd)

join the severed end of the vas directly to the epididymis, which is where the sperm are stored (it's a tubular structure on the top of each testis).

You don't say when your partner had the vasectomy, and timing could make a difference. Research shows that the more recent the vasectomy, the better the results. As many as eight out of ten men are able to make their partners pregnant if they have their reversal within three years of their vasectomy, but this figure drops right down as time goes on. If it's a gap of 15 years, the chances are no higher than three in ten.

The first step is for your partner to get advice from his GP, who can make a referral. Then the method of reversal and its chances of success can be discussed with him, together with any possible drawbacks or side effects. Side effects of the reversal are usually short lived, and are mainly the risk of discomfort for the first days after the operation. After the op, he'd be given advice on bringing a sample of semen for assessment, to see if healthy sperm were reaching the ejaculate.

Assisted reproduction

THE METHODS

This term refers to methods that bring sperm and egg together without sexual intercourse. Assisted reproduction includes:

- ▶ *intrauterine insemination (IUI)*
- ▶ *in vitro fertilization (IVF)*
- ▶ *intracytoplasmic sperm injection (ICSI)*.

IUI

IUI involves timed insemination of sperm directly into the uterus. The woman may be known to be ovulating, or her ovulation can be stimulated with drugs (tablets, injections or both). Stimulating the ovaries increases the risk of a multiple pregnancy, and current UK guidelines recommend IUI only in an unstimulated cycle.

IUI gives the sperm a helping hand on its journey; it's an alternative to IVF if the man has a low sperm count, and is used when a couple have unexplained infertility. Better results have been seen when IUI is combined with fallopian sperm perfusion, when the sperm is mixed with a larger volume of fluid before the sample is inserted.

IVF

IVF starts with hormone treatment to prevent you from ovulating naturally, followed by further treatment to induce ovulation again and to make you produce more than one egg. The use of these drugs has the same possibility of side effects as above.

Some clinics and specialists offer 'mild IVF', which uses a lighter dose of drugs to stimulate ovulation, and which affects the body less. One embryo is transferred. This, practitioners say, reduces the risk of side effects and the risk of multiple pregnancy. Research so far shows it takes more 'mild' treatments to be successful, and not all doctors agree it's the best option. Time will tell if 'mild IVF' becomes more popular or not.

The eggs you produce are then retrieved from your body by a needle, via the vagina. The process is guided by ultrasound, so the surgeon can see on the screen where the needle is going. You are sedated during this procedure and you should feel very little pain. Your partner produces sperm by masturbation and ejaculation, and the sperm is collected and mixed with your eggs in a vessel at the laboratory – not actually in a 'test tube'.

The eggs and sperm are observed, and any fertilized eggs are incubated for up to six days as they develop. The embryos – fertilized eggs – are then studied carefully to see which ones have developed as they should. One or two (in most clinics it's no more than that) are then placed into the uterus.

You will also have hormone drugs (progesterone or human chorionic gonadotrophin) to boost your body's chances of allowing the embryo to implant – without implantation, you're not pregnant.

The National Institute for Health and Clinical Excellence (NICE – see p. 106) reports that IVF success is linked with your age.

▶ *For every 100 women who are 23–35 years old, more than 20 will get pregnant after one cycle of IVF treatment.*
▶ *For every 100 women who are 36–38, around 15 will get pregnant.*
▶ *For every 100 women aged 39, around 10 will get pregnant.*
▶ *For every 100 women aged 40 or over, around six will get pregnant.*

You're more likely to succeed if you've been pregnant or if you've had a baby before. A body mass index of between 19 and 30 means a better chance of success, and you're advised by NICE that, if you drink more than one unit of alcohol a day, consume caffeine, or you or your partner smoke, your chances are also lowered. Increasingly in the UK and elsewhere, donor eggs are used to increase the chances of successful IVF in women over 40.

Insight

The cost of treatment, including the cost of assisted reproduction, is always high, unless you are able to be a health service patient (and the criteria for this may vary and only offer limited attempts). You will also need to be prepared to add in other costs, such as time off work.

Q&A

IVF at 40?

Q. I'm 40, and my partner is 43. We've been trying to get pregnant for four years. We've been told there's now nothing but IVF to try – there's no real explanation for the fact

I can't get pregnant, except that my periods have always been irregular and in the past two years this tendency has been even more obvious. I don't know if we should give IVF a go, or two goes, or three goes. I feel we're at a crossroads, and we need to decide now or never.

A. You're probably already in touch with a counsellor if you have been having fertility investigations – it would be helpful to explore your feelings once more at least. You probably know that IVF in women over the age of 40 using their own fresh eggs does not have a very good success rate. The UK service BioNews.org.uk reports a study from the US showing that 37 per cent of women treated with assisted reproduction technology using their own eggs when they are below the age of 35 had a live birth. This compares with 31 per cent of women aged between 35 and 37; 21 per cent of women aged between 38 and 40; 11 per cent of women aged between 41 and 42; and just four per cent for women older than 42.

Fertilization of donor eggs followed by embryo transfer may be something to discuss, as this is less affected by age. The problem is that donor eggs are in short supply.

ICSI
ICSI has many similarities with IVF, but the sperm is helped to fertilize the egg by being injected directly into it. It's a procedure that's used if the man has no sperm in the semen but does produce sperm (in this case, sperm are harvested directly from the testes). It's also sometimes offered if IVF has failed to create a pregnancy.

Other methods
There are other procedures of assisted reproduction which have been tried in the past, and which may still be available in clinics, but which some specialists believe are not as effective as was once thought. These include Gamete Intra Fallopian Transfer (GIFT). The 'gametes' are the egg and the sperm, and each of them are

placed in the fallopian tube. This method can only be used when there is at least one unblocked tube. It's done under general anaesthetic. Fertilization may then take place. The procedure may be offered to women who have not had success with IVF.

The process ZIFT is the same, except the egg is fertilized outside the body as in IVF, and the resulting zygote is placed in the tube.

You should expect your clinic to share with you the research behind the treatment on offer, their own results, what the cost is going to be (if you are having private treatment), and what the risks might be. Clinics are not all the same, and you should, if you can, shop around by being open about costs and options. Don't be afraid to ask questions. Do your research by asking other fertility contacts what their experience has been, and how they have been treated not just medically, but whether it has been done with kindness and respect.

THE EXPERIENCE

Assisted conception is never an easy procedure, however it's done. It can be painful, uncomfortable, time-consuming and disheartening. It's an amazing technical and medical advance of course, and many, many much-wanted babies are born every day to grateful parents. But the longed-for road to conception, pregnancy and ultimately parenthood is hard for each and every one of those parents.

A study carried out by researchers based at Harvard Medical School put it very well: 'The medicalization of infertility has unwittingly led to a disregard for the emotional responses that couples experience, which include distress, loss of control, stigmatization, and a disruption in the developmental trajectory of adulthood.' In other words, the necessary input of doctors and investigations, and the way they have to interfere and to a certain extent, take over their patients' most intimate lives, is upsetting and prevents people from leading a normal, adult life. (From a study carried out by Beth Israel Deaconess Medical Center, Harvard Medical School, and published in *Best Practice and Research into Clinical Obstetrics and Gynaecology*, April 2007.)

Don't underestimate the side effects of the drug treatment that's part of getting you to ovulate at the 'right' time – some women find them very hard to bear. Being examined and treated may be painful at times, and the rollercoaster of emotions doesn't help (see Chapter 15). All in all, it's a physical, mental and emotional challenge, and one it can be hard to acknowledge in public. There's an assumption that negative feelings are to be lived with, or repressed, out of gratitude that something is being done to help you. Couples may find the whole process strains their relationship to the limit, as each member tries to bend over backwards convincing the other there is no blame attached, especially if tests have shown where a problem lies.

Your specialist clinic will offer counselling, sometimes as a condition of treatment, and it's a good opportunity to explore the sometimes quite deep feelings you may be experiencing around your treatment. It's also a chance to consider the future, what information you will share with any future child or children, or with any children you or your partner already have, and how you will express what's happened. Keeping big, life-long secrets about your child's biological origins – and making sure the people around you who know what's happening and keep them too – is exhausting and draining. It also doesn't work forever. So talking over the ways you can be honest and open with your child as he or she grows is a useful preparation for you.

Insight

Assisted conception is not an easy or very successful process – most attempts do not result in a pregnancy, although success rates are improving all the time.

Transferring one, two, three… or more?
A multiple pregnancy, even twins, is not normally a desirable outcome of any fertility treatment, speaking clinically (what you feel about it is a different matter, of course). Twin pregnancies

are risky, and triplet pregnancies even more so. It's for this reason that current regulations in the UK limit the number of embryos implanted in a woman. The current limit is two for a woman under the age of 40, and three if she is over 40.

Planning for the future

FREEZING

Sperm and embryos may be frozen for future use, and this saves time later if further procedures are done. It also means that the age of the woman is 'preserved', and older eggs are not being used as time goes on. Egg freezing is not at a useful stage yet, though it's just possible this will change in time (see p. 21).

SURROGACY

Surrogacy allows another woman to become pregnant, with a baby that may be wholly genetically someone else's, or not. It is legal in the UK, though payment beyond expenses is not. Commercial surrogacy is available in other countries, where women are paid to carry a pregnancy, but there are issues about who is the legal parent in the UK.

Straight surrogacy is also known as traditional surrogacy. It uses the egg of the surrogate mother and the sperm of the intended father (or donor sperm). It can be done by IVF in a clinic, but it's not necessary – artificial insemination can take place effectively and safely at home (see Kim's story).

Host surrogacy starts off in a clinic, where the egg of the intended mother is fertilized with the sperm of the intended father (or with donor sperm).

Surrogacy is a huge step for everyone involved – and it's not at all clear that our society has got itself sorted out about what the implications are. Parents need to decide how to tell their children about their origins, and explanations are needed for the existing children of the surrogate. The whole issue speaks to us about the meaning of family, being related, the importance or not of biological link. You also need to feel OK about all of this before going ahead.

Surrogacy UK says on their website:

> *You have to be 100 per cent comfortable with the whole situation. Imagine the heartache that can occur when intended parents and surrogate mothers find out that they do not get along after conception has occurred. Once the pregnancy has started, there is no going back. Nine months can be a very long time if you don't have a good relationship. This may sound daunting, BUT surrogacy can and does work beautifully.*

www.surrogacyuk.org

Case study – Kim

I spent nine years trying to become pregnant, and then a year ago, we decided to find out more about surrogacy. It was our last hope. Now, just a year later we are three months away from holding our baby.

We went along to a meeting at Surrogacy UK, to see if this would be an option for us. Through the organization, we met Kim and Mick who already have three children, and after a few more meetings, Kim offered to be a surrogate for us. It's just coincidence they share our names, as my husband is called Mike! We all got on so well – now we feel we are a part of each other's families, and it feels so right to be doing it this way.

It wasn't going to be possible to use my eggs, which meant there was no question of embryo transfer, and so we decided to do it ourselves – no clinic or hospital, just Kim and Mick's home. Kim knew when she was most fertile, and we all met at their house. My husband Mike ejaculated in private, and he then put the semen into a little cup (called an Instead Softcup, available over the internet) which he then gave to Kim. Kim and Mick then went into

(Contd)

their bedroom, and Mick helped Kim get the Instead cup inside, which held the semen in place close to her cervix. She kept it in all night.

Amazingly, it worked the very first time, and we were all so thrilled when Kim announced she was pregnant.

All the way through, she has made it clear she does not think of the baby as hers – we talk about it as 'my baby' and we have discussed every aspect of the birth and afterwards. The hospital where she will give birth knows about our situation, and Mike and I will be there when Kim gives birth. I am planning to breastfeed and I have researched adoptive lactation. I'm hoping to build up a milk supply, supplemented with donated breast milk, in time for when the baby arrives.

There are formal and statutory procedures to go through, to ensure that Mike and I become the baby's parents. We've gone through this very carefully and everything will be above board and legal. Social services in our area have to be notified when we bring the baby home too.

I really don't feel it's important that the baby doesn't have my genes, yet I think it's important to Mike that she does (we already know the baby is a girl). Adoption was something I would have considered very seriously, but Mike was not fully certain that it was something he would feel comfortable with.

When Kim has the baby, she will hand her to me, and I can't wait for that moment – it's been quite worrying up until now, as Kim had some bleeding earlier on, and we hardly dared hope things would continue to go well. Now, though, I can buy baby things and get the house ready for our daughter and it's all such an exciting time. I'm now allowing myself to look forward to the reality of actually having a child. 95 per cent of me feels 'it's going to be all OK'.

(Update: three months after this interview, Kim and Mike went home with their new daughter.)

DONOR SPERM, EGGS AND EMBRYOS

Donor sperm has been used for many years, either in IVF or as part of donor insemination (where the donor sperm is introduced into the prospective mother's uterus). Sperm is donated for a fee, and frozen in a sperm 'bank'. Donor sperm is used when the prospective father is unable to produce effective sperm, or if his partner is 'hostile' to his sperm. It's also used by single women and lesbian women, who don't have a male partner.

A donor's identity is, or rather was, kept private. Recent legislation in the UK now permits children created by donor sperm to trace their biological father, when they reach adulthood.

In the press – Donor identity

In April 2005, donor anonymity was banned in Britain, and the impact was both immediate and dramatic: donations of both sperm and eggs plummeted. From the age of 18, all donor-conceived children now have a right to know the identity of their genetic parents. This means that if you donate sperm or eggs you must be willing to be listed on the HFEA (Human Fertilization and Embroyology Authority) register, which means you could face someone turning up in 18 years' time and asking: 'Are you my real mum/dad?' This has led to the flow of would-be donors abruptly drying up, and is causing widespread panic in the infertility industry. The bold fact is that if you need donor eggs and sperm these days, and no one you know will help you, you're going to have a very hard, possibly very expensive, time getting them.

'The Price of Life' by Viv Groskop, *Guardian*, 13 April 2007

Despite recent changes in legislation, the HFEA – the UK regulatory body for fertility services – reports that sperm donation is still far more common than egg donation. However, the number of egg-donated babies is rising all the time, as the science of it improves. Just 24 egg-donated babies were born in 1991 but in 2004 the number was 535, and over 1100 in the year 2006–7 according to the HFEA.

Donor eggs are a more complex proposition, biologically speaking. The eggs are fertilized by IVF and inserted into the host, and the prospective mother continues with the (hoped for) pregnancy. Again, the donor's identity can be revealed to a child in the future.

Donating eggs is not a simple procedure, medically or socially. It's sometimes done as a sort of 'bargain' – a cycle of IVF in a private clinic is given to them, by the clinic, in exchange for a donation of eggs (and eggs would be removed anyway, as part of the IVF process). Obviously these would be eggs from a young, healthy woman. These eggs would then be available for a woman who cannot produce her own eggs, or who is too old (40 plus) for IVF to be likely to succeed with her own eggs.

In other circumstances, egg donation is done purely altruistically, by women who want to help other women. Only expenses are allowed.

Donor embryos are sometimes created in the course of IVF, when a couple decide to freeze 'extra' embryos which are then not needed. At present, it's only legal to keep them in storage for between five and ten years. These embryos can be donated to another couple. It's by no means a common procedure, and there are plenty of unresolved ethical and legal questions – as there are around all donor-assisted conceptions.

In the press – Fertility clinics to recruit more lesbians as egg donors for IVF

Fertility clinics are to target lesbians as egg donors after research found they were more likely than heterosexual women to give birth after IVF.

The study, published today, reports that gay women who attended a London clinic were up to 20 per cent more likely to have a baby than their heterosexual counterparts.

It opens the way for clinics to ask lesbians to share their eggs.

Researchers believe the difference between lesbian and straight women arises because most gay women seek treatment for lifestyle reasons, and not because they have fertility problems.

Conversely, most straight women seek IVF because they have problems conceiving.

The study was by the London Women's Clinic in Harley Street.

Dr Kamal Ahuja, its scientific director, said: 'These results are remarkable. This is the first indication that the quality of eggs for lesbian women is better.

'It's also a remarkable turnaround – ten years ago lesbian women weren't all that welcome in fertility clinics. Now that's changed. These women are going to be our saviours. This is evidence that they make excellent patients in egg-sharing schemes – both as donors and recipients.'

London Evening Standard, 9 June 2009

Further treatment pathway

If you've had investigations and checks, appropriate medical and/or surgical treatment and you're still not pregnant, your clinic or doctor will discuss further options with you, such as:

▶ *assisted reproduction with your own eggs and sperm, inside the body (e.g., IUI)*
▶ *assisted reproduction with your own eggs and sperm outside the body (e.g., IVF)*
▶ *assisted reproduction with donated eggs or sperm (e.g., donor insemination)*
▶ *assisted reproduction with donated eggs or sperm outside the body*
▶ *surrogacy.*

These are not sequential – it's not that IUI will be tried before donor insemination, for instance. By this stage of the fertility investigations, it may be clear that your eggs or your ovulation is behind the fertility delay, or your partner has a low or nil sperm count. In these cases, there could be no point in attempting conception without donor gametes.

Q&A

My sister as egg donor?

Q. I've been trying to become pregnant for a long time, and my husband and I feel we want to make sure there's no stone left unturned before we give up – and we have been told that if we continue with IVF, we will need to have a donated egg. My sister has three children and, at 33, she's decided she doesn't want any more. I don't know how to bring up the subject of egg donorship – I'm even scared to talk about it in case she thinks I am hinting that I would want her to donate. If she offered, I am certain I would say 'yes' and my husband feels the same way. But I know it is a big thing for anyone to do, and a huge thing for anyone to ask.

A. Is there a counselling service at the clinic you have been attending? If so, you may feel able to explore this topic with the counsellor. You're right – it is something you and your sister, and your respective partners, would need to discuss before you went ahead. You'd need to decide what to tell any child that was born as a result – genetically, he or she would be the half-sibling as well as the cousin of your sister's three children. In addition, your child would have the right to know his or her genetic background, and secrecy is neither a practical nor a desirable option. This might be fine with the four of you, of course. It's reasonable for you to discuss your need for a donated egg with your sister, if you have been keeping her informed about your fertility investigations – hiding your wish for a donated egg might make her think you would not be interested in her donating, and this might prevent her from thinking about offering. Honesty and openness is probably the best for you all, but you might decide that your relationship with your sister is such that you need to wait for her to offer, rather than ask and have her refuse you.

Q&A

New partner – want a child

Q. How successful is reversal of sterilization in the woman? I had a tubal tie five years ago, and I now regret it. I already have three children. My doctor has not been sympathetic, and points out I had counselling at the time of the operation. I've been told it's unlikely to work. I have a new partner and he has not had children before.

A. It's a shame you haven't met with more sympathy – people's circumstances change and what seemed a good decision and a final decision at the time can look rather different a few years down the line.

It's certainly possible for reversal to be successful and to end in a happy, healthy pregnancy and birth. However, estimating success is hard, because it can depend on what state your tubes are in after the operation. The 'tubes' by the way which are 'tied' are the fallopian tubes, which are not so much 'tied' as clipped (or cut or cauterized – sealed by applying heat). A further method inserts a tiny coil into each tube, and body tissue grows round it, blocking the tube. The modern word for tubal tying is 'tubal occlusion'.

Reversal when the tubes have been clipped is the most successful, but realistically, you need to be prepared for

(Contd)

disappointment – some studies say about 50 per cent of operations are successful, but others are not as optimistic as that.

Another thing you might want to think about is the fertility of your partner. It's relatively simple to check this out (see p. 99), at least compared with an investigative or reversal operation for you, and many doctors would advise you both to ensure your partner has no obvious fertility problems first.

Q&A

Same-sex partner: getting pregnant

Q. Where can I find information about becoming pregnant without a male partner? My female partner and I would like our own children, but there's a lot to discuss, including who's the one who becomes pregnant.

A. There are some great resources these days for lesbian and gay parents, and finding support and information from people who have been in just your situation is likely to help you. A highly recommended book is *For Lesbian Parents: Your guide to helping your family grow up, happy, healthy and proud* by Suzanne M. Johnson and Elizabeth O'Connor (Guilford Press, 2001). The website Family Onwards at www.family2000.org.uk has some good articles as well.

The biology of becoming pregnant without a sexual relationship with a man is pretty straightforward, unless there are any underlying fertility issues. Because sperm is pretty resilient, and remains 'fresh' and usable for days, a sample of semen can be inserted in the vagina in whichever way you find it comfortable and convenient (see Kim's story earlier in this chapter).

THINGS TO REMEMBER

1 *One or more diagnostic investigations may also be treatment for you – the tests for fallopian tube patency (openness) can unblock them if this has been a problem.*

2 *Surgery may be able to treat some conditions like fibroids, adhesions and endometriosis.*

3 *Endometriosis can interfere with fertility; however, many women with endometriosis conceive and have trouble-free pregnancies.*

4 *In polycystic ovarian syndrome (PCOS), there is a wide spectrum of symptoms, and probably most women who have a mild form of the condition don't notice they have it.*

5 *Fertility drugs can stimulate your body to produce and release an egg from the ovaries.*

6 *Sometimes, you may find the use of drug therapy produces side effects you don't like.*

7 *In men, blockages (such as a cyst or cysts) in the testicles inhibiting sperm flow can be removed surgically.*

8 *A low sperm count, or if sperm are seen to be poor in quality, may be overcome with a surgical process called sperm recovery, which obtains sperm direct from the testes with fine-needle aspiration.*

9 *Assisted reproduction means methods that bring sperm and egg together without sexual intercourse.*

10 *Assisted reproduction techniques are more likely to succeed if you've been pregnant before.*

14

Another baby... or not?

In this chapter you will learn:
- *how fertility problems can emerge or re-emerge after a successful pregnancy or pregnancies*
- *about the emotional impact of secondary infertility*
- *about the decision to have one child only, or to accept things as a fait accompli.*

Secondary infertility

Although having one child only is not uncommon at all, there is an expectation that once you've had one baby, you're bound to want another one. You may or may not feel the same desire to conceive again, but if you do, what happens when it doesn't happen, doesn't happen straight away, or if you end up unable to have another child? The term 'secondary infertility' applies to anyone who has successfully had at least one baby, and then finds they can't seem to have another one.

Causes of secondary infertility are broadly similar to the causes of primary infertility – and any investigations into it, and solutions to it, will follow on in a similar way.

Even if you conceived easily the first time, that won't necessarily be the case next time round. First time may have been luck – you hit the right time in your cycle perhaps, both of you were at peak fertility fitness at the same moment, or it just happened.

Maybe you weren't aware of some underlying condition that tests this time round make apparent. Or perhaps you have since developed a condition that impacts on your fertility.

You are, naturally enough, older than you were when you first became pregnant – if this tips you into the over-35 age group, that physiological drop in your fertility we discussed in Chapter 1 could be the cause of a delay. If you have a new partner, are not managing to conceive, and he has not had children before, investigations would probably start with a sperm count for him, as this makes the most logical sense.

If you needed medical or surgical help, or assisted conception with your first pregnancy, it's likely the same process will be needed again (depending on the reasons for it – unblocked fallopian tubes should remain unblocked, for example). On the other hand, if no reason was ever found for your fertility problems, it's possible you could become pregnant spontaneously this time – quite a few parents have been surprised that way.

Insight

Some secondary infertility is a natural consequence of being older and hitting the age group where conception is inevitably less easy.

EMOTIONAL TURMOIL

If you're facing a problem conceiving again, and you already have one (or more) children, you can end up coping with a mix of pressures and feelings, some of them contradictory, and not all of them logical:

▶ *expectations from friends and family that you are bound to want to have another child*
▶ *worries that your child will suffer without siblings*
▶ *direct queries from people who ask outright if and when you are going to have another baby*

- *guilt that you are asking 'too much' of fate, especially if you went through a 'journey' to have your child – maybe you should be happy with what you've got?*
- *lack of sympathy from other people if you seek help – they either think you don't need the help, just a bit of patience, or that you are taking up the time of a clinic from someone else who really needs it*
- *if you have a new partner, expectations that you will want to seal the new union with a child, and direct questions about it*
- *sensitivity to your new partner's feelings, and the assumption on other people's parts that the problem must be down to him*
- *jealousy (or at least envy) of others who seem to have as many children as they want, when they want*
- *a possibly surprisingly strong yearning for another baby, as intense as the feeling you had first time round*
- *a dread of repeating the process you went through before, if it was unpleasant*
- *fear that it won't work this time*
- *uncertainty about how far and how long to persist with treatment or 'trying'*
- *uncertainty about how long to wait before seeking help, especially if you feel time is running out.*

Getting support and having the chance to share your concerns and worries will help a lot. There are specialist discussion boards on the internet aimed specifically at people in just this very situation. It's also important to share your concerns with your doctor or fertility clinic, and to get an informed view of when it would be reasonable, if at all, to get some medical input.

Return of your fertility

If you have no underlying fertility problems and you are still in a relatively fertile age group, your fertility is likely to come back after your first child's birth when you stop breastfeeding, or when you stop breastfeeding frequently – this is very variable, with some women re-starting their periods within weeks, and others not for many months if the baby is still breastfeeding, even if the baby is eating a lot of solid food. If you don't breastfeed, or only breastfeed for a very short time, you may find your periods (and therefore your fertility) return in a few weeks – anything from six weeks onwards.

If you're not menstruating, you're almost certainly not ovulating. Breastfeeding is designed to delay your fertility, as it's nature's way of ensuring you only have one dependent child at a time. The hormones involved in lactation put a break on the production of oestrogen. But if you want to be pregnant again, you have to make a choice if you are still without periods. You can:

▶ *continue breastfeeding, and leave it up to time and nature for your fertility to return, recognizing that this may not be for a while*
▶ *cut down the frequency of your breastfeeding, to see if this 'invites' the return of your periods*
▶ *stop breastfeeding completely (but do this gradually).*

Insight

Using a fertility/ovulation kit can help establish when your fertility returns.

Q&A

Breastfeeding and fertility

Q. I'm still breastfeeding my baby, who is aged 14 months. I have not yet had a period. We would like to have a second baby, but I have been told I won't get pregnant while I'm breastfeeding. What are the real facts about the impact of breastfeeding on fertility?

A. Looking at the situation from the other end, that is, from the 'don't want to be pregnant' situation, breastfeeding is an efficient contraceptive for at least the first six months

(Contd)

postpartum, as long as the baby is fully or almost fully breastfed, and as long as the woman is not having periods. There is an international guideline called the 'Bellagio consensus', which outlines 'LAM' – the 'lactational amenorrhoea method' of contraception – and acknowledges that if the guidance is followed, the 'failure' rate of this method is two per cent. In other words, if 100 women used LAM for a year, 98 of them would not become pregnant (and, of course, two of them would). It may be that LAM can extend beyond the first six months if the woman's periods have not yet returned, but the research on this is not as robust.

The 'amenorrhoea' bit of LAM means absence of periods, and it's this that's the strongest measure of potential fertility; it could well be that the fact you've not got your period again is a strong indicator that you're not yet fertile again. (Not having periods while doing any breastfeeding, even just once or twice a day, is still on the normal spectrum, by the way. Other women find their periods return a lot sooner – that's normal too).

Once your periods return, you can be pretty sure you're able to become pregnant again. If it's important to you to become pregnant soon, you could consider reducing the amount of breastfeeding you are doing, and see if this makes a difference. It is possible to become pregnant while breastfeeding before your periods have returned though – sometimes, ovulation happens before menstruation returns. A few women have been surprised that way!

Q&A

Caesarean section and subsequent pregnancy

Q. I had a caesarean section with my first baby, and I've heard different opinions on when it would be OK to try to conceive a second child. My mother told me her doctor advised her to wait three years, but I don't want to wait that long.

A. The old idea that you should wait came about because it was thought you ought to allow the incision in your uterus to become stronger with longer-term healing, but current advice is that today's smaller incisions heal fast and firmly, and there's no need to be that cautious. Three months is the usual advice, it seems, but do check with your own doctor or midwife first.

Insight

Having a caesarean section with your first baby does not have to mean a repeat section for subsequent births. It depends on what the original reason for the caesarean was.

Deciding one is enough

There is a prejudice, if that's not too strong a word, not against only children themselves, but against the notion of having only one child. There may be some 'inherited memory' here – with child mortality high for most of human existence, having one child only was no way to ensure your family lived on, or that you would be looked after in your old age. There may also be some romanticizing of the family – if family is good, then lots of family must be better, whereas the truth is that individual variations mean that having a sibling or two is no guarantee of friendship or even any relationship at all beyond childhood.

Being an only child, and having an only child is a different experience from having siblings or having two or more children. But it's not necessarily worse. Accepting and even embracing the upsides of having a single child, for yourselves and for your child, is the only way forward, if this is what you decide to do.

Case study – Anne

After my daughter was born, I went through hell with serious physical problems related to a prolapsed bladder and uterus due to the labour and birth. I'd always assumed I would have at least one other baby, but I was not in a condition to even think about it. In the end, I was referred for a hysterectomy. We thought long and hard about it, but it really was the only way left to resolve the painful and crippling effects of my condition. When I had it done, I was so relieved – the pain went, and I realized it was the right decision. There was a time when I felt very sad though. I was grieving for the child I didn't have. It took a while to come to terms with that, but now, three years on, I'm totally comfortable with it. I just get annoyed when people make assumptions. Someone said to me: 'Oh, are you not going to have another child?' in a sort of accusatory way, as if somehow this was something I ought to do.

Case study – That Question!

Are you an only child?
Haven't you got any brothers or sisters?
My heart sinks
my stomach turns
I fear the next remarks
I expect your mum and dad spoil you,
don't they?
I smile wanly
What can I say?
If I say yes –
heads nod knowingly

If I say no –
eyebrows raise ever so slightly
in disbelief.
I can't win
so I say nothing
I look down, shuffle my shoes,
and feel ashamed.

by Dr. Bernice Sorensen, therapist and counsellor,
who researched the experience of being an only child.

Insight
'Only' rhymes with 'lonely' – but they don't mean the same thing!

THINGS TO REMEMBER

1 *Secondary infertility describes fertility problems that emerge when trying to conceive a second or subsequent child.*

2 *Causes of these problems may be similar to the causes of primary infertility.*

3 *Assisted conception may need to be repeated.*

4 *Breastfeeding may affect the return of your fertility.*

5 *Waiting several months or more after a caesarean section is no longer thought to be necessary.*

6 *The decision to have one child only may appear to be questionable by other people.*

15

The emotional journey

In this chapter you will learn:
- *how your relationships with your partner, family and friends can be affected*
- *how waiting to conceive has an intense impact on your feelings*
- *how support can enable and encourage you.*

Trying to get pregnant

People lucky enough to get pregnant without a long delay, without investigations, tests, treatment, disappointments and heartbreak, are envied by couples who go through all that and more in the quest to have a child. It's not just a series of physical hurdles – the emotional and psychological impact is one that's often underestimated. Coping with the 'waiting to be pregnant' time can challenge the strongest relationships, test the most long-lasting friendships and family ties, and lead to feelings of jealousy and anger towards people who don't share the same problems.

Treatment for infertility is not always gracious or gentle. You have to wait, queue, answer endless questions, and have your sex life dissected. When you have sex with your partner, at the back of your mind you're wondering 'Is this going to be it?' or even 'What's the point of this?' Not all doctors are wonderfully sympathetic, not all clinics are warm and welcoming; in both the public and private sector, standards vary a lot.

Crass, unfunny and unthinking remarks from people can astound you as well as hurt you. 'Oh, no babies? I bet you're having fun trying!' is a common one. Or 'Well, maybe God doesn't want you to have a baby' is another. 'Perhaps it's nature's way,' says someone else. 'Have you found out whose fault it is yet?' might ask someone who knows you're going for treatment.

Support groups can be a real help, not just with the sometimes daunting task of getting information and comparing clinics and treatments, but as a 'safety valve' where the really deep, dark feelings of despair, and the negative feelings towards others, can be expressed. Internet forums offer a great way of sharing support and all the major parenting sites have them, as well as websites dedicated to fertility issues only. You have to learn the jargon to take part – internet fertility language is unique and like all specialist vocabulary, it's a way of creating a group identity – maybe just what you need when you are feeling alone and misunderstood.

Insight

There may be a support group connected to your clinic if you are undergoing tests and checks. This can be helpful and supportive.

Internet jargon

Some of the terms you'll see on internet boards include:

AF = 'aunt flo' i.e., period
BD = 'baby dancing' i.e., having sex
BFP = Big Fat Positive on the pregnancy test
BFN = Big Fat Negative on the pregnancy test
DD = dear daughter
DH/DP = dear husband/dear partner
DS = dear son
EP = ectopic pregnancy
HSG = hysterosalpingogram (see p. 103)

IRL = in real life i.e., not in cyberspace
IYSWIM/IYKWIM = if you see/know what I mean
OPK = ovulation predictor kit
pg = pregnant
TMI = too much information
ttc = trying to conceive
2WW = the 'two-week wait' between ovulation and the time you
can take a pregnancy test and trust the result.

Real life experiences shared

These are from UK Parents Lounge on the internet:

▶ *'I think the waiting is the worst part of all. I always know I'm pregnant within a few days of having sex, but I never get a positive test until nearly a week after my period due date. Even though I know I am, I still find the waiting really hard and end up wasting money on tests.'*

▶ *'Thursday this week is the anniversary of me losing our last baby at 15 weeks, this whole business is so, so hard. I never thought I would feel like this. One of my employees just announced she's pregnant and she was on the pill. I only found out yesterday and I'm devastated. I couldn't stop crying yesterday.'*

▶ *'I'm feeling like such a failure. I never dreamt it would ever be this hard. I had no idea how this would feel, and how every month my heart feels like it has been ripped out of my body.'*

▶ *'I have one beautiful child, but yet I still feel incomplete. I just want this more than anything else in the world, and I've hit a wall. There is nowhere else to go; it's left in nature's hands. I hate not being in control.'*

▶ *'I know I am opening myself up to ridicule, but I have no one IRL to talk to about any of this. Everyone around me is getting pregnant and having babies, and I don't think I can take any more "So when are you going to have another one?" questions.'*

▶ *'When trying for our first I fell pregnant the first month, so when we decided to try again I expected it to be just as easy... was I wrong! The second took nearly a year and it was heartbreaking every month when AF came.'*

▶ *'I went to the docs for tests which all came back OK, then one month I said to DH I've had enough I want some time off trying IYKWIM. We had a fab month and I went back to being totally relaxed and enjoyed sex again (it didn't feel like a chore). Guess what – that month I fell pregnant. I don't know if it was just luck, but it happened for us, so it will for you!'*

▶ *'I haven't used any contraception since August 1998 and only have DD. Not likely to have another either, despite desperately wanting one. DD will be starting school in September and I've already got the 'you'll have to have another to keep you busy' line. If only... I know I'll hear it more frequently too, come September.'*

▶ *'I still can't quite believe it since the timing seemed to be all wrong, but my cycles have been really messed up the last couple of months, so I guess anything's possible. I'm going to do another test on Tuesday just to be 100 per cent sure, but I'm just really glad my first instincts were right! I could tell as soon as I'd conceived practically, but after three BFNs I felt a right idiot – guess it was just too early!'*

▶ *'I'm sat here in tears. You may remember that recently I had another miscarriage (five in total). I desperately want more babies, and it's devastating each time I lose one. Anyway, I use another parenting site and today three ladies have found out that they are pg again; none of them are happy about it or want them. It's just so unfair. I can't even post on that site today, as it is just too difficult when I'm having such a hard time (3 m/c since DS2) and they get pg just like that and don't even want it.'*

▶ *'Sorry, but just needed to put it into words. We still have another month before we can ttc again, although we have been naughty really and not done anything to prevent it happening sooner, not that it has, but you never know.'*

▶ *'I've just bought a test, but I daren't use it until I get home from work. AF is a day late. I'm never normally late – but I do feel like it will come any minute, but that's how I felt last time I was pg. It's probably a false alarm, but I can't stop myself getting my hopes up.'*

Insight

Trying to get pregnant may not be a happy time when it takes longer than you planned. You may be surprised at how angry and resentful you feel.

Case study – Lilian

I lost a good friend over all of this. She became pregnant for the second time, and I couldn't get over the fact that here I was, still trying, and she managed it, twice, with no problems. I know it was irrational, I know it's not her fault we were having problems... but I couldn't help it. I didn't get in touch with her at all, and didn't return her calls. I couldn't face her. Maybe I should just pick up the phone and say 'Sorry', but I'm not ready to. I feel guilty, but I just can't help it. It's a lot easier to just keep what I feel to myself, and not have to hide it if I see her.

Q&A

I'm jealous of her pregnancies

Q. My oldest and best friend is pregnant with her third baby, and I'm still trying to become pregnant with my first. I've been through unsuccessful treatments, and it's starting to look less and less likely we will have a baby. It's now becoming a difficult issue between us – when she told me she was pregnant for the third time, I could hardly bring myself to say 'Congratulations'. I really love her two boys, and I honestly wish her joy and delight with her family – I babysit, my husband and I take the boys on outings and I appreciate how much my friend 'shares' them with us. But this third baby seems a baby too far. The irrational side of me thinks stupid things, like 'How can she be so greedy?' and 'It's not fair – I would be a great mum, and probably better than her, and how can she manage three when the other two are still so young?' I hate these thoughts, but they're getting in the way of our friendship.

(Contd)

A. That's so sad for you – it's likely your friend is aware of the whole sensitive area of her becoming pregnant so easily, while you are still struggling. She'd have to have a heart of stone not to have some inkling. How about letting her know your ambivalence – the good thoughts you have, which are genuine, and admit to some of the bad thoughts which come from your disappointment? You don't need to spell out the thoughts you have about her timing or her skills as a mother, but just say there is a part of you that resents her third pregnancy for reasons connected with your sadness at not being pregnant yourself. Ask her for support and understanding. A good friend will give it. In time, you will accept her third baby, and probably even welcome him or her as another in your brood of 'nephews and nieces'.

Insight

Don't lose good friends out of resentment – good friends will understand if you share what you feel about their pregnancy while you are still trying.

Irritating and maddening remarks

▶ *How about the helpful friend who says: 'I'll loan you my husband – he just looked at me and I was pregnant!'*

▶ *From the well meaning, but nonetheless annoying sister-in-law, who is 8.5 months pregnant with her second child: 'Just stop trying'.*

▶ *'Just have lots of sex, then you can't go wrong!' I hate that comment. My brother-in-law said that the other day, Mr Know-it-all.*

▶ *I hate it when my husband's family says: 'Aren't you all ever going to have children? You're not getting any younger you* know!' If I hear: 'You're trying too hard' one more time I am going to scream!

▶ I'm an atheist. My friends know this. And yet, a very religious friend of mine says these things (of course – she's in her 20s… and had no problem conceiving her second, which is due soon):

1 Be patient. God moves in mysterious ways.
2 Things happen for a reason.
3 God is testing you.

ARRRRGH!!!

▶ I have the sister-in-law who wouldn't tell me she was pregnant with her fourth child (she had to wait until my husband got on the phone) because she didn't want to 'hurt' my feelings. The 'pity' thing is really getting to me!

▶ Went to dinner with three other couples – two are pregnant and started trying after we did. I had recently had a miscarriage and was already having a hard time seeing them, knowing they were still pregnant. We had two tables pushed together and the way it worked out the two couples that were pregnant were at one table and we were at the other table. Well, one girl kept calling their table the 'special' table because they were both pregnant and couldn't drink alcohol. I wanted to just go and cry!

▶ This is from the doctor and nurse who did my HSG, while the tube was inside me and we were all looking at the screen.

Doctor: 'Well, this was never a problem for me.'

Nurse: 'No, it certainly wasn't.'

[They both giggle.]

Nurse: 'You should see his huge family.'

From www.tryingtoconceive.com

Case study – Pattie

You know what gets to me? When I see a pregnant woman smoking. I want to go up to her and snatch the cigarette from her mouth, and tell her she's abusing her baby. Here I am, I have given up everything I enjoyed in my life, just about, to get ready for pregnancy. I have had all the tests, and the prodding and the intrusion in my life, and willingly, to have a baby. And to her, her baby's health and safety seem to mean nothing. I don't understand it, and it makes me so angry. I have to look away.

THINGS TO REMEMBER

1 *Fertility issues can cause problems in relationships.*

2 *Treatment and investigations can be difficult to cope with.*

3 *Other people's reactions and comments can be hurtful.*

4 *Support from people undergoing similar experiences can be helpful.*

5 *Learn the jargon for internet forums!*

6 *Some women become resentful and jealous of other women's pregnancies.*

Glossary

Blastocyst The embryo on days 5–6 after fertilization.

Chromosome Present within the nucleus of every cell, containing the genes.

Cryopreservation The technical term for freezing and storing eggs, sperm or embryos.

Donor The giver of gametes i.e., a woman who donates eggs or a man who donates sperm.

Donor insemination Placement of sperm from a donor into the woman.

FSH Follicle Stimulating Hormone (see p. 27).

hCG Human Chorionic Gonadotrophin (see p. 40).

Embryo The fertilized egg.

Embryo transfer The transfer of one or more embryos to the uterus.

Endometriosis The condition due to which cells that normally make up the lining of the uterus appear on the outside of the uterus and other pelvic organs. It can affect fertility.

Epididymis Tubes situated outside the testicles, which store sperm.

Fallopian tube(s) Tubes connecting the ovaries and the uterus.